define the
relationship

A CANDID LOOK
at BREAKING UP,
MAKING UP, AND
DATING WELL

Jeramy and Jerusha Clark

BEST-SELLING AUTHORS OF *I Gave Dating a Chance*

Praise for
Define the Relationship

"*Define the Relationship* takes a refreshing approach to dating by shining light on the subtle pitfalls couples face today. In an entertaining, honest, and life-changing way, Jeramy and Jerusha address things such as good communication skills, how to guard emotional as well as sexual purity, and what it means to have a God-centered self. Jeramy and Jerusha Clark fill a huge vacuum in Christian resources on dating by writing this book."

—DR. LORI SALIERNO, speaker, author, and founder
   of Celebrate Life International

"*Define the Relationship* is tailor-made for serious-minded, sincere young people who want to build quality long-term relationships. Loaded with examples and experience, Jeramy and Jerusha masterfully walk through how to communicate in relationships at every level—from first dates to final breakups. A valuable resource, not only for dating but also for building strong foundations for communication in marriage."

—PAUL FLEISCHMANN, president of National Network
   of Youth Ministries

"Jeramy and Jerusha not only have a heart for God, they have a heart for helping young people build healthy relationships. In this helpful book, they offer tips for communication that can set any relationship on the right course. *Define the Relationship* helps you learn communication skills that lead to honesty, openness, and true intimacy—and that's the way God desires our relationships to be defined."

—LAURIE POLICH, speaker, author, and youth ministry professor

define the
relationship

A Candid Look
at Breaking Up,
Making Up, and
Dating Well

Jeramy and Jerusha Clark

WaterBrook
Press

DEFINE THE RELATIONSHIP
PUBLISHED BY WATERBROOK PRESS
2375 Telstar Drive, Suite 160
Colorado Springs, CO 80920
A division of Random House, Inc.

All Scripture quotations, unless otherwise indicated, are taken from the *Holy Bible, New International Version*®. NIV®. Copyright © 1973, 1978, 1984 by International Bible Society. Used by permission of Zondervan Publishing House. All rights reserved. Scripture quotations marked (KJV) are taken from the *King James Version.* Scripture quotations marked (TLB) are taken from *The Living Bible* copyright © 1971. Used by permission of Tyndale House Publishers, Inc., Wheaton, Illinois 60189. All rights reserved. Scripture quotations marked (MSG) are taken from *The Message.* Copyright © by Eugene H. Peterson 1993, 1994, 1995. Used by permission of NavPress Publishing Group. Scripture quotations marked (NASB) are taken from the *New American Standard Bible®.* © Copyright The Lockman Foundation 1960, 1962, 1963, 1968, 1971, 1972, 1973, 1975, 1977, 1995. Used by permission. (www.Lockman.org). Scripture quotations marked (NLT) are taken from the *Holy Bible, New Living Translation,* copyright © 1996. Used by permission of Tyndale House Publishers, Inc., Wheaton, Illinois 60189. All rights reserved. Scripture quotations marked (Phillips) are taken from *The New Testament in Modern English, Revised Edition* © 1972 by J. B. Phillips.

Details in some anecdotes and stories have been changed to protect the identities of the persons involved.

ISBN 1-57856-592-8

Copyright © 2004 by Jeramy and Jerusha Clark

Library of Congress Cataloging-in-Publication Data
Clark, Jeramy.
    Define the relationship : making up, breaking up, and dating well / Jeramy and Jerusha Clark.—
1st ed.
        p. cm.
Includes bibliographical references.
    ISBN 1-57856-592-8
    1. Man-woman relationships. 2. Interpersonal relations—Religious aspects. 3. Rejection
(Psychology) 4. Interpersonal communication. 5. Personality development.
I. Clark, Jerusha. II. Title.
    HQ801.C532 2003
    306.7—dc22

                                                                                                2003018892

Printed in the United States of America
2004—First Edition

10 9 8 7 6 5 4 3 2 1

For two men of character
who have served God faithfully,
shaping the lives of many—including our own:

Ted Montoya
and
Eric Heard

Contents

Acknowledgments

Our deepest thanks to the entire WaterBrook Press team, particularly Don Pape and Steve Cobb, who took a chance on us, encouraging and enabling us to write. Thank you for your understanding during tough periods and your willingness to trust God with the timing of *DTR*.

To our editor, Elisa Stanford: Your fresh perspective, keen observations, and effective cuts molded this book into what it is. We thank God for your skill and dedication.

We are ever grateful for Brian Aaby, one of the biggest supporters of our family and ministry. Brian, you always have an encouraging word, a laugh to share, and an exhortation. Thank you.

God has gifted us with Spencer and Rona Clark, parents whose prayers and loving support exemplify faith and joy, even through their own struggles with illness.

Thank you to JAC and LeAnn Redford, who generously gave of their time, energy, and resources to help while we wrote. Our love bug is thankful for her Mimi and Babbo, and so are we.

Uncle Tom and Aunt Penny Anderson, we cannot express what your presence in our lives means. Our first few months in Escondido (and in your house!) have been defined by true fellowship with you.

For amazing help in very limited time, we would like to thank Lorraine Pintus. You believed in us and in this book. Your relationship with the Lord is inspiring.

Thank you to Heather Caliri, a colleague and friend, whose faithful friendship and encouragement to persevere remain invaluable.

And thank you to Dennis Keating, who willingly and graciously shared from his wisdom and experience. It's great to be a part of the EFCC family and the pastoral team you lead.

Above all, we would like to thank our Lord and Savior, our best friend, the reason we live and write: Jesus Christ. You taught us that trials can define our relationship with each other and with You. You have allowed us the immense joy of relationship with our own little ones, and You gave us the vision and words for this project.

Introduction

You've seen it a million times... Fade from black... Cue music and lights... Enter the hero's abode...

The house teems with energy, and Daniel mills about, taking pleasure in his guests and the fact that today is *his* birthday. Yet something is missing.

Daniel took extra time getting ready for this evening. He dressed with care, choosing a pair of dark jeans (wanting to appear both casually comfortable and polished) and a sweater. Yet something is still missing.

Suddenly there she is.

Daniel catches only a glimpse of her from across the crowded living room. Her dark hair falls alluringly about her shoulders, her smile radiates, and her eyes dance with life as she laughs. Oh, what a laugh. His heart pounds with one question, *Who is she?*

Glasses clink and the music swells as he's captured in that single glance. She moves aside with a couple of girlfriends, heading for the drinks on the patio. *Who is she? Why is she here at his birthday party when he doesn't even know her name? Why does it feel as if she's been here all along?*

Staring through the French doors, he holds her in his gaze. She laughs again.

Pressing on with head tilted downward to avoid eye contact with anyone who might stop his progress toward *her,* Daniel moves quickly, with purpose he's known few times in his twentysome years. He finally senses *it,* and nothing can stand in his way.

There she is. Seated on the brick retaining wall, sipping a soda, and laughing again. Daniel takes a moment to compose himself and rehearse a hundred minidialogues in his mind. Then he sees his chance...

Her girlfriends drift into conversation, and she rises, crossing the lawn to refill her soda. Daniel meets her at the drink table. He smiles as winsomely as he can with his heart racing. He doesn't even know what he says, but it must be clever because she laughs and allows him to serve her a drink.

As he passes the cup to her, their hands brush, and he senses something he's never felt before. *Magic.* All he did was touch her hand, and yet he knows instantly that he has come home. Hasn't something been missing? Until now, maybe…

They flirt. They tease and play. Their conversation bounces from topic to topic, and they pause every once in a while to laugh and momentarily stare at each other incredulously. How could they share so much, so immediately?

The party goes on around them, but it means nothing to this couple. As the hour grows late, her girlfriends come back, making the "Are you coming with us?" motion. Daniel pipes in straightaway, "I'd be happy to take her home."

And so he does. He walks her to the door, he takes her face in his hands, and he kisses her tenderly and knowingly. A kiss that stops time. A kiss that reorders time.

At that moment he knows that he will spend the rest of his life with her. *It*…no, *she,* is no longer missing.

THE MISSING PIECE

You might not expect a book on Christian relationships to begin with a scene like this. Why, it's straight out of some chick flick. Just add a group of girls playing "This Kiss" over and over while eating Ben and Jerry's ice cream and drinking hot chocolate. "A kiss that stops time"? Is this for real? Does stuff like this really happen?

Let us clue you in as to why we opened our book this way: The scene exemplifies our culture's typical portrayal of falling in love. Tweak the circumstances slightly and you have the script for hundreds of films, sitcom subplots, and novels. Even if the hero and heroine face seemingly insurmountable odds, love almost always triumphs. When lovers don't overcome, when they die or must endure separation, we're brought to tears by the injustice of it all. Shouldn't they get a chance at "happily ever after"?

Yet most of the time in the media, the couple in love makes resolving the challenges of life and love look easy. Their problems are solved in two hours or less on the big screen, and a mere twenty-two minutes in the television world. And what's behind this formula—besides the millions of dollars needed to make the season premieres and movies we clamor to see?

If we're honest, we recognize that behind the gloss and the "kiss that reorders time" is a *lie.* Or a pack of lies, really. Many of us have been snookered into expecting that the ideal relationship follows this pattern. We've been tricked into believing first that falling for someone, that "love at first sight," is the ultimate experience we can expect and desire, and second, that it's easy to fall and then stay in love. Doesn't love conquer all?

The thrill of the first glance. The chase. The wondering and watching. The fluttering stomach, the racing pulse, the sweaty palms (okay, so maybe movies don't show that too often). And you can't forget the *romance*—the lighting, the playful banter, the music that sets everything in a perfect, dreamy realm. As we view such scenes over and over again, we're set up to crave this, to dream about it, even to expect it.

Falling for someone and then staying in love is supposed to be easy, right? The most natural thing in the world! The best thing that could happen to anyone! That's what we've been told since we started watching Disney princes and princesses fall in love "once upon a time." We've also been inundated with the message that "love is all you need." We've been sold on the lie that, no matter what, "My heart will go on." Many of us have been convinced that some*one* can and will be "everything you want, everything you need, everything you wish you could be."

What we *don't* see on-screen are the times a couple faces crossroads where tough decisions have to be made. Where love fades and the two people wonder, *Is this person really who I thought he (or she) was?* We don't see the daily grind of misunderstandings and hurt, growth and ache that is a part of being in a relationship.

Maybe you're arguing in your mind that believers shouldn't really have to sort through our culture's deceptions. After all, we know the truth. You're right: We are *supposed* to know the truth. But the reality is that we're not immune to the power of cultural lies simply because we're Christians.

And when we dismantle the deceptions, we can see that these lies have just enough truth in them to send us—Christians who desire to honor God as we relate to the opposite sex—on a search for something that doesn't even exist.

So What Is the Truth?

People need and crave love on a number of levels. Psychologists have concluded that love is not *all* that humans yearn to experience—we also long for security, self-worth, and significance, among other things. Yet love interfaces with all these things. Its centrality in our search for fulfillment cannot be denied.

But we didn't need the psychology departments of major universities to tell us that, did we? We *feel* it in our inner being. We want to be known. We desire affection and meaningful relationship. We ache to love and be loved.

That hunger motivates and drives a great deal of our thought and actions when it comes to relating to the opposite sex. Friendship is one type of relationship within which men and women enjoy the fruits of love. Loving brotherhood and sisterhood in Christ adds another dimension to the interaction of the sexes. And so does romance.

But the Enemy tries to distort the truth of what love is and how one comes to fall in love. But the truth is, falling in love *is* part of the human experience. Falling for someone, however, was never meant to be the ultimate end. Sometimes it's merely the beginning of a godly romantic relationship that leads to love and marriage.

The Enemy's twisted emphasis on the easy road of "love at first sight," though, has in it enough biblical truth to cause heartache and confusion. We love how Dr. Ed Wheat describes the truth about the first couple who fell in love…at first sight!

> As Christians we can be sure that romantic love is as old as Time itself, for it came into being in the Garden when the first man and woman gazed on each other. We must recognize that it was our Creator who gifted us with the capacity for the intense and passionate emotions required to fall in love. Clearly, God intended for our emotional potential to be fully developed in marriage and to find its fulfillment in oneness with our beloved.[1]

The first man and woman gazed on each other and fell in love with each other in perfect, pre-Fall fellowship. They had been created—uniquely fashioned by the Lord—for each other. They were not only to enjoy each other, but also to establish the institution of marriage, God's perfect design for the fulfillment of romantic love.

When you look at the post-Fall tragedies Adam and Eve endured, you can imagine that it took a lot for them to stay in love, to stay committed to each other. The consequences of sin in relationships are real and challenging.

This probably isn't news to you, but you are *not* in a pre-Fall state of perfect fellowship with the opposite sex. What's more, not all of your dating relationships will be or should be relationships of love or relationships that lead to marriage. The reality is, if you choose to date, you are going to be in relationships that will require more of you than simply falling for someone. If you pin your hopes on the kind of relationship that simply *happens,* you're on the Enemy's ground.

One of the ways the Enemy tricks us into pursuing a false ideal for relationships is by getting us to idolize and go after the relationships that seem instinctual, easy, and in many ways, complication-free. In his book *The Five Love Languages,* Gary Chapman highlights the truth that

the "in love experience"…is on the level of instinct. It is not premeditated; it simply *happens* in the normal context of male-female relationships. It can be fostered or quenched, but it does not arise by conscious choice…. The "in love experience" *temporarily* meets one's emotional need for love. It gives us the feeling that someone cares, that someone admires and appreciates us. Our emotions soar with the thought that another person sees us as number one, that he or she is willing to devote time and energies exclusively to our relationship.[2]

The key word here is *temporarily.* The sensation of "falling in love" or "falling for someone" may fill, sustain, and satisfy, but only for a time. Dr. Chapman continues:

Our most basic emotional need is not to fall in love but to be *genuinely* loved by another, to know a love that grows out of reason and choice, not instinct…. [We] need to be loved by someone who *chooses* to love…who sees in [us] something worth loving. That kind of love requires effort and discipline.[3]

Keep a few words from this quote tucked away in your mind:

- *Reason*
- *Choice*
- *Effort*
- *Discipline*

To experience love that goes beyond merely satisfying temporary needs, we have to do some work. We have to employ reason and make wise choices. We need to exert effort and exercise discipline. Does this truth disappoint you? We don't blame you if it does. The world makes it seem so easy; the media presents a vision that appeals to those of us who want to avoid at all costs things like discipline and reason. But the truth is, these things are to be combined with the "falling for someone" aspects, the romance and fun and delight of relationships. The world gives us only a twisted glimpse, an incomplete picture, of what real love involves.

As God guides your relationships, you'll see the whole truth. You'll also see His strength pouring into you, enabling you to bring reason, choices, effort, and discipline into your interactions with the opposite sex.

This book is about training yourself for godly relationships. It's about tearing apart the lies you've bought into and building your character in truth. It's about working to define your relationships on different levels and at different times so that you can enjoy the freedom and abundant life that Christ came to bring.

WHAT YOU CAN EXPECT

In order to equip you for godly dating relationships that may eventually lead to love and marriage, we need to examine several facets of male-female interactions. We're going to start by looking seriously at the most important relationship you can have and why it defines every other relationship in which you may engage. Then we're going to jump into some explanatory chapters: How do you "define a relationship"? What is a DTR? When should you have one? When should you *not* have one?

We'll look next at the details of defining relationships at different stages: the beginning, the middle, and the end. Since we know that some relationships end in breakups, we're going to take time to analyze how to break up well, as well as how to survive a breakup. We'll also look at a different kind of ending—choosing to have that DTR to decide whether to become engaged.

Then we'll dig into some things that hinder us from maintaining healthy, clearly defined relationships. We'll examine emotions that get in the way and consider how to stay emotionally pure before marriage. Finally, we'll talk candidly about sexuality and its place in godly dating relationships.

We pray that, as you begin to read this book, you will set aside any expectations and allow the Lord to speak to you about these areas. We know firsthand that struggles and questions surround dating relationships. We trust God to use His Word, as well as the stories and experiences He's given us, to mature and bless you as you come to a deeper awareness of the beauty of godly love—the authentic True Love.

Defining Your Most Important Relationship

Recently, our extended family sat around the Sunday dinner table and discussed what the greatest words in the English language are. We were all surprised when we quickly agreed upon the answer. A group of twenty-some people *rarely*—if ever—unanimously assent to anything.

But once someone suggested the three words (together, of course) "I love you," debate morphed into total agreement. These three small words, even when spoken out of context, held a palpable power over the group.

Since it was close to the anniversary of our engagement, we were immediately transported back to the first time we exchanged those words. Both of us were on bended knee, so to speak, because Jerusha had lost her balance when Jeramy pulled the tiny white ring box out of his backpack.

You may be shocked to find out that we didn't profess love for each other until the day of our engagement. But after much consideration and because of our histories of emotional attachments that went too deep too quickly, we had determined that we would be better off if we waited to say "I love you" until we could put a commitment behind those words.

This decision *did* put us in somewhat of a pickle once our relationship started to head down the road to marriage. It seemed silly to verbalize something along the lines of "I'm in like with you." And it sounded strange to say "I like you a lot" when we were so obviously serious about each other.

Still, we respected the power of the phrase "I love you." I (Jerusha) had had a negative experience in one of my earliest relationships when my boyfriend of only a few months called me to claim fervently that he loved me. Not knowing what to do (and admittedly being immature in the ways of dating), I simply hung up the phone.

We can look back and laugh at that now, but at the time it shook me to hear those words used in what seemed like such an inappropriate and flippant manner. Even then, I sensed that it *meant* something to say "I love you." It involved more than I could give at that time and certainly more than I felt.

During high school, I (Jeramy) became involved in a relationship that lasted about two years. I used the phrase "I love you" often, but when the relationship ended in betrayal and pain, the words we'd exchanged seemed empty and false. I realized there had to be something more to "I love you." There had to be a true commitment to back up those words.

But we were talking about our dilemma prior to engagement: We knew that we felt strongly about each other, probably strongly enough to say the words "I love you" and put a solid commitment with them. But our relationship was not yet at that stage, and we wanted to protect ourselves from the possibility of our feelings or situation taking a dramatic turn.

So we talked about what we could say to express how we felt about each other without using those "sacred" words. (We'd love to have a recording of that conversation. It was most likely fodder for great comedy.) We went round and round, not coming up with anything that seemed to fit. The words we put together seemed forced or weak. Finally, Jeramy jokingly suggested that we just say "I...you." It worked. We realized it fit where our relationship was by leaving a space where we knew something more belonged. Almost like an engagement ring, it promised something better to come.

We only used "I...you" for a month or so, and then we were engaged. Some skeptical people may be thinking, *Well, you pretty much said "I love you"; you were really just messing with semantics.* But we weren't. We recognized the force and beauty and truth and *eternity* inherent in the words "I love you." We wanted to savor those choice words only when we knew our relationship was secure enough to contain the power that came with them.

WHAT WE ALL WANT TO HEAR

There are probably few things people long to hear more than "I love you." We even like to hear these words spoken between complete strangers. Think about how many movies (even the action-adventure ones) climax with the main characters proclaiming their love for each other.

No movie is complete without the love plot or subplot. Love somehow makes a horror movie less scary and a war movie more bearable. Knowing that the protagonist has a wife and baby at home motivates us to root for his success. Seeing the young woman who is stalked by a killer held in the strong arms of a boyfriend or husband makes the audience feel more secure about her future. And hearing the words "I love you" spoken—in passion, through tears, *however* they're uttered—brings life and hope and peace.

Some might argue that they'd prefer to hear "You've won the lottery! Yes, the jackpot of sixty-three million dollars is yours" or perhaps "You're the most amazing person I've ever met." But it's almost as if the words "I love you" contain these sentiments within them. This little phrase packs more than three words' worth, that's certain. When someone genuinely says "I love you," it suggests that you are the richest of men or the most cherished of women.

"I love you" does even more than that: The phrase subtly pronounces you—all of you—as good and acceptable. Many people, particularly popular people, struggle with the deep fear that if others *really* knew them or found out what they were *really* like, they wouldn't be so admired after all. The words "I love you" suggest that you are *known* and loved—just as you are.

It's easiest to accept the words "I love you" when you've done something considered worthy of the sentiment. Maybe you helped a friend through an incredibly tough time or ministered to your parents while they were sick or divorcing. Maybe you did something as simple as take out the garbage. If you are blessed to receive the words "I love you" in return, it's relatively easy to believe them to be true. You *feel* lovable, so you must *be* lovable.

If, on the other hand, you have done *nothing* good or, worse, you have behaved terribly and unlovably, it's almost impossible to trust those words. Your spirit responds, "There's no way you can love me. I'm a terrible person. I've hurt you, and I'm selfish and horrid. You can't love me, and I don't love myself."

Somehow, even in the darkest of moments when we feel the most unlovable and awful, we hold out hope that someone could—in fact, *does*—love us. Truly loves us. We want to hear it and know it. We want to feel it: *I am loved.*

Sadly, many single people believe that if they just heard those precious words from someone, the ache in their heart would abate. Somehow the question, Am I loved? would be settled forever. We have seen many people get involved and stay in a relationship simply because it gave them a measure of confidence that they were known and loved and cherished. Ultimately (and you have to stick with us to understand), this desire to be someone's beloved is not bad or wrong. On the contrary, *you (yes, YOU!) were created to be loved—for eternity.* You are beloved. Not only that, but you are *the beloved.* The beloved of Christ. His bride, His eternal love. That's why it's absolutely essential that you define the most important relationship in your life before you get into the dynamics of a dating relationship. When you define your relationship with the Lord, you will know that you are loved—unconditionally and eternally.

WHAT THE CROSS SETTLED

Our hearts ache for unconditional and permanent love just as a hungry man's stomach roars for food: "That distant rumbling from deep within is our restlessly growling soul. It's saying in so many words, 'I'm empty and I want to be filled.' And so we search. We look for something to satisfy this relentless appetite."[1]

The problem is not so much that our souls growl restlessly or that we look to sate that hunger for love. The problem is that we look everywhere except the right place for that love. Our world offers a myriad of choices to numb the ache of a heart desperate for love. Some people turn to drugs or alcohol or food. Some look to exercise, to accomplishment at work, or to the high of extreme sports to meet their needs. And many turn to relationships. People seem to think, *If I could just find the right boyfriend or girlfriend, maybe my appetite for affection would be curbed. Maybe we could get married, and then I'd never have to wonder again if I am loved.*

Relationships seem like the most natural, logical place to turn to find fulfillment for an empty, aching heart. And the truth is that "God has created us with deep cravings in our spirit, especially for relationship.... We hunger to be loved so relentlessly and unconditionally that we won't have to perform for acceptance."[2] God Himself designed us with a hole in our hearts that only an intimate love relationship with Him can fill. He never intended that people should meet our deepest heart needs.

That's why a great dating relationship will not fill the void within us.

Even a fabulous marriage won't fill the gap. Nothing in this world can sat-isfy the yearning within us. C. S. Lewis once wrote, "If I find in myself a desire which no experience in this world can satisfy, the most probable explanation is that I was made for another world."[3] We would add that if you find in yourself a desire for relationship that no relationship in this world can satisfy, the most probable explanation is you were made for another kind of relationship—and you were. You were designed with an empty place that only one relationship can fill. The hole in your heart is God-shaped.[4]

The cross of Christ settled forever the question of whether or not you are loved. Let us repeat that: The cross of Christ settled *forever* the ques-tion of whether or not you are loved. You are. In their book *Experiencing God,* Blackaby and King wrote these powerful words: Calvary "is where God clearly demonstrated once and for all time His deep love for me.... In the death and resurrection of Jesus Christ, God forever convinced me that He loved me. The cross...[is] God's final, total, and complete expres-sion that He loves us."[5] Until you have experienced the fulfilling intimacy of an authentic love relationship with Jesus Christ, nothing will satisfy your rumbling and restless soul.

As Ruth Myers affirms, only "the Lord can meet our every need because He is a God of perfect, overflowing love that has no limits."[6] And Psalm 63:3 proclaims, "[God's] love is better than life." Psalm 108:4 de-clares that His "unfailing love is higher than the heavens" (NLT). God can more than satisfy you. He may grant you the blessing of love relationships with other people as well. But you will not *need* those relationships; you will not have to look to them for what they cannot give if you build an intimate love relationship with Jesus. As Shirley Rice says, "Once you've been loved by God, you are loved completely, and you do not need to grasp anymore."

As hard as you may try to make a dating relationship strong, healthy, and godly, nothing in your life will be right, including your relationships with others, unless you develop a real and personal relationship with Jesus Christ. Alexander McClaren prayed, "O God my strength, if I fix my happiness on anything less stable than the heavens, less sufficient than You, sooner or later I will lose it. If my life entwines around any earthly prop, some time or other my prop will be plucked up.... Therefore I choose to entwine the tendrils of my life around You." You can entwine your life around the earthly props of human love relationships. But sooner or later you will see that those props fall down or fail. Only God's love is as stable, as perfect, as complete as the love you seek.

So we pray with Paul, "May your roots go down deep into the soil of God's marvelous love; and may you be able to feel and understand, as all God's children should, how long, how wide, how deep, and how high his love really is; and to experience this love for yourselves" (Ephesians 3:17-19, TLB). To experience God's love for yourself, you need to define or re-define your relationship with Him personally.

In the next few pages, we're going to talk to two different groups: those who want to begin a love relationship with Jesus and those who may have started that relationship but sense that God has something more for them. If you don't know where you fit, we suggest that you read both sections. If you have an established relationship with the Lord, you may want to skip to the latter section, where we'd like to present you with some ideas to consider.

"Whole and Lasting Life"

When Jesus died on the cross, God welcomed us into a relationship with Him. His sacrifice saved us from certain destruction: "This is how much God loved the world: He gave his Son, his one and only Son. And this is why: so that no one need be destroyed; by believing in him, anyone can have a whole and lasting life" (John 3:16, MSG). At the cross, Jesus gave Himself that you might have life.

We've written the remainder of this book to those who have "whole and lasting life"—those who have trusted Jesus Christ as their personal Savior and confessed Him as Lord of their life. Yet we know that some of you reading this book know *about* God but don't yet *know Him*. You can read all the self-help books you can get your hands on to try to strengthen your relationships, but the ultimate need of your heart will remain unmet if you have not first chosen an intimate love relationship with God. This book, too, will mean little to you if you have not experienced the love of God that saves and frees. Will you consider right now accepting His completely satisfying love? If you sense a hunger in your heart to begin a love relationship with Jesus, take a few moments with us…

First, read Romans 3:23: "For all have sinned and fall short of the glory of God." (Trust us. This *is* the right place to start, though it may seem a harsh beginning.) No one is perfect. If you doubt us, just ask anyone who lives with you if they think you've led a perfect life thus far. Or consider this: How many times do you have to kill before you're a murderer? Once. How many times do you have to steal before you're a thief? Just once. Or lie to become a liar? Again, once. How many times do you have to sin to be a sinner? *One time only.* **A love relationship with God begins with admitting that you're not perfect and recognizing that sin has a steep price tag.**

Now read Romans 6:23: "For the wages of sin is death." The cost of sin is death. That's the price you pay to do something wrong. The Bible tells us that when the first man and woman sinned, death entered God's perfect creation. Sin brings death to us all. This is what we'd call very bad news!

Yet it's only half the story. We haven't gotten to the good news yet. The second half of Romans 6:23 reads, "But the gift of God is eternal life in Christ Jesus our Lord." Acting out of love for you, Jesus paid the price for your sin. Romans 5:8 proclaims, "But God demonstrates his own love for us in this: While we were still sinners, Christ died for us."

The two greatest words in the Bible may be "but God…" Those two words reflect the grace of the gospel. We are sinners and sin leads to death. *But God* did not leave us in our sin. *But God* gave the gift of everlasting life through His Son. We'd call this very good news! And it gets even better: Your cost for this gift? Nothing. It is yours free of charge. **A love relationship with God involves simply accepting His free gift.**

Those who accept the free gift of salvation take these final steps: They confess and believe. Romans 10:9-11 promises, "If you confess with your mouth, 'Jesus is Lord,' and believe in your heart that God raised him from the dead, you will be saved. For it is with your heart that you believe and are justified, and it is with your mouth that you confess and are saved. As the Scripture says, 'Anyone who trusts in him will never be put to shame.'"

There's no trick to it; there's no gimmick. The Scripture does not say, "You *might* be saved" or "God *might* enter into a love relationship with you." Anyone who trusts in Jesus *will* be saved and will *never* be put to shame.

In a love relationship with God, you believe in Jesus and confess Him as Lord. If with your heart you truly believe that Jesus is who He claimed to be—the Son of God and the Way, the Truth, and the Life—and with your mouth you proclaim Him "Lord," the "whole and lasting life" of love Jesus bought at the cross is yours. You will have a relationship with Jesus—immediately. First John 5:12 affirms that "he who has the Son has life; he who does not have the Son of God does not have life."

If you have made the decision to begin a love relationship with Jesus, you have the life! You've begun the greatest journey a person can take. In John 10:10 Jesus says, "I came so they [including you!] can have real and eternal life, more and better life than they ever dreamed of" (MSG).

There are so many amazing things in store for you as you get to know Jesus better—more than you can possibly imagine. But you're going to need some help along the way. And this book isn't the kind of support you need first.

If you have just defined the most important relationship of your life, what do you do now? Go to Disneyland? No. Well, maybe to celebrate. But you also need to grow in this new love relationship. Please tell another Christian about your decision. Ask him or her to help you find a strong, Bible-believing and Bible-teaching church. Seek out a pastor or mentor who can help nurture your intimacy with Jesus.

We're overjoyed to have shared these moments with you. We pray that you might seize the "whole and lasting life" you've chosen in Jesus, loving Him with all you are.

TIME TO RENEW?

Those of you who chose to come straight here most likely consider yourselves Christians. But we don't want to assume that all of you feel that your love relationship with Jesus is authentic, alive, and thriving.

Maybe as you read this chapter you realized that you've been trying to fill the void in your heart with things other than God. Maybe you've fallen away because of various distractions or a busy schedule. Perhaps you've allowed sin to creep into your life, and it has left you feeling distant from Jesus. Or maybe a dating relationship has started to become more important to you than cultivating your passion for the Lord. Perhaps you've never made your faith your own. Or maybe you've let spiritual activities or pursuits such as Bible study, prayer, and church services eclipse God's personal presence in your life. Any of these things can leave you feeling stale, dry, and stagnant in your faith. The void in your heart will ache when you're not right with Jesus.

If you see yourself described in the previous paragraph, wouldn't you like to rekindle the most important relationship in your life? to get back to Jesus, your first love, so that you might also learn to authentically relate to others?

Begin redefining your relationship with Jesus by examining your heart. Second Corinthians 13:5 exhorts us to "Check up on yourselves. Are you really Christians? Do you pass the test? Do you feel Christ's presence and power more and more within you? Or are you just pretending to be Christians when actually you aren't at all?" (TLB). It's so easy to fall into pretending in the Christian faith. When you're in a great church, a strong Christian family, and circle of believing friends, you might be tempted just to ride on the faith of others.

So as you consider redefining your relationship with Jesus, first ask yourself, **Is my faith truly my own?** As author Len Woods wrote,

"Borrowed Christianity" is what you see when people talk *about* God and do stuff *for* God, but they rarely talk *to* God or spend time *with* him. It's a handed down kind of spirituality, a circumstantial kind of faith. It depends on special events or certain people. In its good moments it can appear healthy and vibrant. In its bad moments it is shown for what it often is—a weak and worthless faith.[7]

Is Jesus a real person to you? a person with whom you share a deep and intimate love? a person in whom you invest your life—your time, your energy, and your resources? Have you determined what you believe, or have you inherited faith from your parents, your pastor, or a girlfriend or boyfriend?

If you've never made your faith your own, the hunger in your soul will gnaw at you until you find satisfaction. You may seek to sate the hunger in all the wrong ways. "Borrowed Christianity" destroys all kinds of relationships between members of the opposite sex because people with an inauthentic commitment to loving Jesus cannot relate to others in healthy, godly ways.

When I (Jerusha) went to college, I realized that I'd been living on a borrowed faith for some time. I'd gone to church since I was a little girl, and I knew a lot about God. Deep down I also knew that a relationship with Christ was the most significant thing in my life. But I had never surrendered my life and my heart to God in an intimate, personal way. I'd never chosen to spend time praying or nourishing my soul with God's Word. I had been living in a Christian home with parents who loved Jesus, and I'd been going to a church where lots of people around me loved Him as well. It seemed enough to borrow from their faith and experience spiritual highs sporadically and vicariously.

Going to a university fifteen hundred miles away from home, away from the church I had grown up in, and away from the relationships that had propped up my faith, I began to realize that a borrowed faith would not satisfy me. On my own for the first time, I chose to firmly establish my most important relationship. I chose to nurture a living, loving relationship with Jesus. As I grew in my faith, I started to see my relationships with others—including my relationships with men—change. My desires and behaviors began to align with what Jesus wanted for me. I finally knew God's love in a personal, authentic way, and that knowledge changed my life.

If you sense that you've borrowed faith up to this point, *now* is the time to make your faith in Jesus your own. If you haven't a clue how to do that, ask a person who you know has a true love and passion for Christ to talk with you about it. My transformation began when a mentor modeled for me how to love Jesus and be renewed by His love. This woman of God showed me how she could spend time with Christ—in prayer, in His

Word, in fellowship, in service, and in worship. As you spend time with the Lord, you will also begin to experience a deepening love for Him.

Some of you may be thinking, *I already have a quiet time every day* or *I'm really involved in church, but I still feel distant from Jesus.* To you we pose the question, **Are duties and circumstances hindering your authentic love relationship with Jesus?** In his book *Toxic Faith,* Stephen Arterburn describes those who have

> a destructive and dangerous relationship with a religion that allows the religion, not the relationship with God, to control a person's life.... The toxic faithful find a replacement for God.... Acts of religion replace steps of growth. A facade is substituted for a heart longing [and] forms a barrier between the believer and God, leaving the believer to survive with a destructive addiction to religion.[8]

It's possible to do all the "right things"—to spend time in prayer or in Bible study, to serve in the church, or to serve His causes—yet never personally and passionately give yourself to Jesus. Oswald Chambers warns against becoming a "Christian" whose god is your "godly habits"— prayer, Bible study, quiet time. He admonishes us to watch that we do not say, "This is my time alone with God," when in reality it is "time alone with our habit." Chambers continues, "There is a vast difference between devotion to a person and devotion to principles or to a cause.... Discipleship means personal, passionate devotion to a Person—our Lord Jesus Christ."[9]

Nothing can or should take God's place in your heart—not even the things He's asked you to pursue and given you to enjoy. Focusing on those pursuits alone can lead not only to a "toxic faith," but also to an inability to relate authentically to others. If you've allowed religiosity and habitual ritual to define your relationship with Jesus, you'll build relationships with others that are grounded in accomplishments, objects, and circumstances.

The only way to break the cycle is to offer yourself to Jesus without the pretension and props. Come to Him just as you are and ask *Him* to redefine your life. Let Jesus strip your walk with Him down to fundamentals and then let Him build it anew. He will do so faithfully because He longs for authentic communion with you. He died to enjoy that privilege.

Whether you've allowed a relationship or godly habits to take God's place in your life, whether you're living in sin or living with a borrowed faith, redefining your relationship with the Lord means returning to Him: confessing where you've been, asking for His forgiveness and renewal, turning back to Him in genuine prayer and devotion, and making Him first in your life.

The Great Priority of Life

Secure in your relationship with the Lord, you will be able to engage in relationships with others free from the question, Am I loved? As a married couple, we ourselves do not know that we are loved or worthwhile because we say "I love you" to each other every day. Instead, because we know Jesus, we are confident that we are *completely* loved whether or not a source of human love fades or fails. No human relationship could survive if its purpose were to settle the matter of our belovedness. That weight is too great. We are flawed, broken humans who cannot perfectly love one another as we need and long to be loved. So the two of us have made it our primary goal in life to define and constantly redefine our most important relationship: our relationship with the Lover of our soul, Jesus Christ.

Nothing is more important in life than learning to nurture an authentic love relationship with Jesus. Matthew 22:37-38 proclaims, "Love the

Lord your God with all your heart and with all your soul and with all your mind. This is the first and greatest commandment." This statement boils life down and sums it up. Nothing is more essential.

We once heard the story of a football player named Vernon. A big guy with a big heart, Vernon played with passion even in practice. One afternoon, during a particularly intense play, Vernon gave everything he had and got blindsided. Knocked flat on his back, he was out cold. The other players and coaches quickly surrounded Vernon, trying to figure out what damage might have been done. When Vernon opened his eyes, everyone breathed a sigh of relief.

But he was completely dazed and confused. Someone asked him if he knew what day it was, and he responded, "I don't know. All I know is I love Jesus." Others asked him about his family, his friends, and his beloved 1967 Chevy. He answered every single question with "I don't know. All I know is I love Jesus." In his stunned state, Vernon clung to only one thing: His relationship with Jesus was his core priority and what he valued most in life.

The rest of this book will be about defining your relationships with people, particularly people of the other gender. But think about this: If you were blindsided and knocked out cold by a relationship, what would that experience reveal about the greatest priority of your life? Would you—like Vernon—declare, "All I know is I love Jesus"?

Jesus settled forever the question of whether you are loved. You do not need to grasp for love from anything else—relationships with the opposite sex included. Listen to Him speak to you today—and every day—the words "I love you." Believe His words of love to be true. Learn to love Him back. Then you'll be ready and free to define healthy, godly relationships with other people.

What Is a DTR?

As Andrea stepped onto her college campus for the first time, she felt a rush of excitement followed directly by a wave of unbearable nausea. The anticipation that had been building inside of her over the summer culminated now as she surveyed the place that would be her home for the next four years. Andrea managed to locate her room and find places for most of her things. She thought it a bit curious that her roommate hadn't shown up yet. Wild horses couldn't have kept Andrea off the grounds at 8 a.m., when her trusty orientation-week booklet reported that freshmen could begin moving into the dorms.

Though nearly crazy with curiosity, Andrea had to wait until the next day to meet her roomie. Cheryl showed up just after breakfast, and she seemed entirely unlike the other freshmen girls—confident, at ease, and unconcerned with the rest of the crowd. Andrea found out soon enough that this was because Cheryl *wasn't* a first-year student. She was entering her second year and had been placed in the freshmen dorm by lottery.

That night—Saturday night—was the welcome banquet, followed by a mixer, during which all of the campus activities were to be presented in the hopes of recruiting fresh blood. Andrea looked forward to this time because she wanted to be involved with both campus life and a Christian organization of some kind. She felt thankful to have a roommate who was experienced and could give her the lowdown on the different clubs and associations. Andrea had been delighted to find out that Cheryl was also a believer, and the two had already agreed to encourage each other to get up for church on Sundays. It probably shouldn't have shocked Andrea when Cheryl told her she wouldn't be attending the banquet and party. After all, it was designed for freshmen. Disappointed, Andrea asked what that night would hold for Cheryl.

"Well, it's time for James and me to have a DTR," Cheryl explained matter-of-factly, as if Andrea would know exactly what she meant. Andrea hated feeling naive. She tried to phrase her question as lightly and innocuously as possible: "I'm sorry. What did you say?"

"James and I. We've been on a few dates over the last month, and now it's time to DTR." Cheryl turned from her tiny vanity mirror and, seeing Andrea's expression, understood the source of her confusion.

"Andrea!" she exclaimed apologetically. "I completely forgot. I hadn't heard of DTR until I got here either. It means a 'define the relationship' talk. It's kind of the catch phrase among Christians here."

Andrea nodded to show she was following, but she actually had no idea what a "define the relationship" talk could entail.

But then Andrea hadn't done a whole lot of dating in high school. She'd gone to dances with different guys and had a boyfriend for a few months during her senior year, but things hadn't gone so smoothly when Andrea told Philip that she had chosen an out-of-state school. She remembered being startled at the depth of his feelings. He had imagined they were going to stay together once graduation passed and the summer faded into a new school year. Andrea wondered now if a "DTR" talk would have benefited her and Philip. Maybe then she wouldn't have blindsided him with the breakup and they could have stayed friends.

It didn't take Andrea long to figure out just what DTR was all about. She soon connected with the campus ministry Cheryl was part of, and the two of them spent almost every Friday night hanging out after the meet-ing with a group of guys and girls. The subject of DTR came up often among these new friends.

Pretty soon Andrea had carved her own niche in the circle of friends and started to spend more time with a couple of the guys on other nights. By second semester, these friendships led to invitations for casual dates, and before long she needed to give the whole DTR thing a try.

Andrea had been around the group long enough to study DTRs at lots of different stages—like when a couple first started going out and wanted to decide if they'd be exclusive, or when a couple had been together awhile and needed to redefine boundaries and expectations, and even when couples had a "final" DTR that ended in a breakup or an engagement. So far she'd seen a handful of breakups, and one couple had set a wedding date.

The common theme was that these relationships had been shaped from the beginning by the principle that clear communication of feelings, emotions, and expectations—in other words, DTRs—were valuable for building, maintaining, and even ending a dating relationship well.

Andrea had observed how easy it was for things to get confusing or for people to avoid spelling out what they really felt and intended. This confusion naturally led to a lot of frustration, a bunch of game-playing, and some gruesome breakups. She felt relieved to have a tool like DTR at her disposal so she could avoid these pitfalls, which seemed so common to the dating experience. But at the same time, she felt lost when it came to the nitty-gritty of defining a relationship.

Those problems aside, Andrea had also noticed that there appeared to be certain unspoken rules for DTRs on her campus. You couldn't, for instance, wimp out and do it over the phone. Not only did a DTR have to happen face-to-face, but most people went to the same place to DTR.

It was a running joke that you knew what was coming when someone wanted to go to Beans 'n' Cream to talk.

Beyond that, the couple DTRing had to pray together during their conversation at least once, and it was expected that other people would be praying for them during this time as well. After all, both parties would've talked through the details with their girl or guy friends before the meeting, so those friends would already know what to pray for specifically.

But Andrea still wondered, *What does a healthy, godly DTR look like?* As Andrea told us later, she skinned her knees quite a few times in the process of discovering what constituted a good DTR. When we told her we were writing a book about the subject, she could barely contain herself: "I am so excited that someone is finally writing about what to do with DTRs. You don't know how much I wish this had been written four years ago!"

Andrea and many others graciously shared their stories with us in hopes that you might steer clear of some of the pain and confusion so often associated with dating. With clearly defined relationships, with a couple functioning on the same wavelength, and with the shared awareness that people's emotions are precious and should be treated that way, many of the dating dilemmas singles face can be avoided.

So, to begin, focus with us on what a DTR is—and what it is not.

DEFINING OUR TERMS

On Andrea's campus, DTRs might have been accepted as the norm, but the term was still confusing. What *is* a DTR anyway? A DTR is a communication tool used to assess a relationship's strengths and weaknesses. It helps two people determine their shared level of interest as well as their intentions for the relationship's future. A DTR can be used either to set the course for a couple or to end the journey. It can and should be utilized to maintain a healthy relationship during its natural growth process.

Consider your options when it comes to dating relationships. Perhaps you've always played something like the "he loves me, he loves me not" game, plucking the petals off flowers to determine where a relationship is headed. That seems a little futile for something as perplexing and intense as opposite-sex relationships.

Most people fall somewhere between these two extremes: At one end of the spectrum is the haphazard, reckless, undefined, go-with-the-flow mentality; and at the other end is a continual monitoring and reevaluating of the relationship's development. Let us give you a glimpse into the relationships of four couples. See if you can determine which couple utilized DTRs most effectively.

Don't Force It

Consider Hayley and Michael, who never regarded where their relationship was headed as a big deal. They didn't think it was important to talk about emotional or physical boundaries, and they sure didn't want to talk about their feelings for each other. Wouldn't that be forcing things or quenching the natural flow of the relationship? At the least, a conversation like that would be uncomfortable, and it could end up in hurt feelings.

So Hayley and Michael let things progress in what they thought was the natural way, and pretty soon they were spending every spare minute together. They completely checked out of their other relationships and began to see their interest in other things—hobbies, work, church—wane.

Both had assumed that since they were Christians, they would agree on where they should be in a physical relationship. But night after night they found themselves struggling with what felt good versus what the Holy Spirit was convicting them about concerning right and wrong.

Though they cared deeply about each other, they could sense that something was amiss. This wasn't the way relationships were supposed to be. They carried a weight of guilt and concern.

It wasn't that they didn't want to honor God with their relationship. They never intended to stray from Him or elevate their relationship above Him. Hayley wondered how things had gotten out of hand. Michael kept asking himself, *Does this mean I have to break up with her?*

No Channels of Communication

Perhaps you've observed couples like John and Julie. After a month or so of dating, Julie began to wonder if John liked her as much as she liked him. She tried to find out, asking his friends and dropping hints during their dates. At first John didn't notice much, but after a while this undercurrent of constant questioning—which he saw as Julie's insecurity—started to really annoy him.

In an effort to keep things peaceful, Julie tried pleasing John with physical affection. But this, too, frustrated him because he wanted to be more intimate with her and yet knew that wasn't what God desired.

Soon John started looking for ways to spend less time with Julie and more time with his friends. Julie felt that her only option was to make herself more desirable and attractive to John than anyone else. She became so consumed with him that all she could think about was how he felt—or didn't feel—about her.

She couldn't talk to him about it. They'd never had a conversation like that before. Besides, she noticed that any time she brought "them" up, he quickly changed the subject and sometimes even rolled his eyes in obvious aggravation.

Julie thought she and John were perfect for each other. They used to have so much fun. Now things just felt heavy.

I Want to Know...Now

And then we have Danielle and Eric. They started things off by talking about what they expected and hoped for in the relationship. Eric couldn't believe how freeing that conversation was. Some of the tension and mystery of dating evaporated, and he was excited to know that Danielle was as interested as he was in pursuing a physically, emotionally, and spiritually healthy relationship.

A week or so after their talk, though, Danielle brought up "the future." Eric was happy to share what he was thinking—which wasn't much—and listened as Danielle poured out a master plan for their dating relationship: when they could start holding hands, when they should meet each other's families, when they should consider kissing, and so on.

Eric thought this plan was a little extreme and wondered if it was a joke. When he asked Danielle, she laughed and said, "Of course. Did you think I needed to know *now* if you were going to try to kiss me before our fifth month?" They dropped the subject.

But the very next week, Danielle asked Eric if anything had changed since their first talk. She sensed he was drifting from her, and she wanted to make sure that they stayed on the same page.

Eric assured her that nothing much had changed, though the whole conversation left him with a sour taste in his mouth. He ended their date early with the excuse that he had to get ready for a presentation the next day. When he got home, that sour taste just wouldn't go away.

Things came to a head two days later, when Danielle wanted to hash through a telephone conversation they'd had the night before. She just didn't get what Eric was saying and had to go over every detail multiple times, asking a ton of questions and always reading more into things than Eric imagined anyone could.

He felt sick to his stomach now. It had been so great to talk about their relationship a month ago when things were just launching. The discussions had given him a sense of freedom and peace. But these last three talks had knocked the wind out of him. He didn't think he could handle her bringing up their relationship again.

They Had Always Been Able to Talk

Wendy and Blake are our final couple. They had dated other people before meeting each other, and they had both come to the conclusion that the key to maintaining a healthy relationship was to communicate well.

So, after a few dates, Blake initiated a conversation with Wendy. They both acknowledged they enjoyed spending time together and wanted to see where the relationship would go. They decided not to see anyone else in the meantime.

A couple of months later, Wendy approached Blake, and they talked about what to call each other. They decided that "boyfriend" and "girlfriend" fit and didn't freak either of them out.

For Blake the labels meant it was time to lay some ground rules for the physical aspect of their relationship. Wendy and he had an intentional conversation about this topic. They agreed to commit this area of their relationship to prayer and to find someone to keep them each accountable.

As they spent more time together, Blake and Wendy recognized that they needed quality time apart just as much as they needed quality time together. So they set some guidelines as to how much they'd talk on the phone and how often they'd go out one-on-one.

About eight months into their relationship, Wendy started to spend more and more time with her girlfriends. She felt less like hanging out with Blake when he called for a date. It wasn't that anything was significantly *wrong*. But after eight months she knew she didn't want to marry Blake. She also realized it wasn't fair to continue in the relationship, so she asked Blake to come over for dinner that weekend.

The conversation was hard, and Blake was hurt in some ways, but they had stayed up-to-date with each other, and he had to acknowledge that Wendy's hesitancies didn't come out of left field. When he got up to leave, they hugged and promised to approach each other if there was anything that remained unresolved after tonight. They had always been able to talk openly.

DTR = Communication

Wendy and Blake's relationship was obviously the healthiest and most desirable, and they didn't even stay together forever. What made their relationship successful was the open channel of communication. They established this early and kept it unblocked by communicating often.

Communication is the most important part of DTR. You could even say it's the entire *definition* of DTR. All manner of terrible things happen when people don't communicate well. Disagreements and misunderstandings drag on. Questions are left unanswered. False assumptions remain unchecked. Confusion and concern rule instead of peace and trust. Wes Roberts and H. Norman Wright, authors and relationship experts, wrote in their excellent book *Before You Say "I Do,"* "Communication is to love [relationships] what blood is to life."[1] In other words, if communication isn't flowing well in your relationship, your whole relationship will suffer.

Communication is more than talking. Talking involves sending a message. Communication includes the reception of that message as well. The goal of communication is to bring two people to a common and clear understanding.

We communicate with more than words. Wes Roberts and H. Norman Wright elaborate:

In our communication we send messages. Every message has three components: the actual content, the tone of voice, and the nonverbal communication.... [These] three components of communication must be complementary. One researcher has suggested the following breakdown of the importance of the three components. The percentages indicate how much of the message is sent through each one...

Content / 7%

Tone / 38%

Nonverbal / 55%[2]

Does this shock anyone the way it did us? *Most* of communication is not what is said but what accompanies the statement. Expression, stance—all of our nonverbal cues make up more than half of the message we are trying to communicate or receive.

It has also been proven that "if there is a contradiction between what a person hears and what they see, they'll probably be inclined to believe what they see."[3] So the nonverbal component of communication, the greatest of these components, is the most important when it comes to discerning what a person meant and determining what the other person heard.

It's not difficult to see why communication is the first and most important principle of DTR. If the goal of a healthy relationship is to bring two people to a shared vision of where a relationship is and where it is headed, proficient communication is a nonnegotiable.

A healthy DTR takes into account all three components of communication. Imagine a breakup DTR during which the person breaking up is holding the other's hand, stroking the other's hair, or sitting close by on the couch. Do you think that the spoken message might be misconstrued?

Something as simple as how you sit or stand, or how you use your gestures or eyes, can significantly alter your communication.

Learning how to communicate within our dating relationships prepares us for marriage, which will be helped or harmed by the health of our communication skills. Dale Burke, the pastor who convinced Jeramy that he needed to take Jerusha out, wrote this in his book *Different by Design:* "If the three keys to real estate are 'location, location, location,' you could say that the three keys to marriage are communication, communication, communication."[4] Bottom line: Beginning with dating and continuing into marriage, communication is central to healthy relationships with the opposite sex.

The equation is simple: DTR = communication. Good communication takes into account both verbal and nonverbal dynamics. With this in mind, let's look at the factors that help make DTR communication successful.

Eight Principles That Guide Healthy DTRs

An entire book could be written about how communication affects the way we relate to others, particularly the opposite sex. We're sure someone could also come up with a book about which aspects of healthy communication best shape an effective DTR conversation. In the interest of providing a concrete definition for defining the relationship, we've narrowed healthy DTR principles down to eight essentials.

1. A DTR Provides an Arena in Which Two People Can Dialogue Positively About Their Relationship

A DTR creates a safe and established forum in which a couple can talk about the many facets of their relationship: misunderstandings, boundaries, guidelines, physical issues, spiritual dynamics, emotional needs, and expectations. Couples often find it difficult to know when to talk about these things. Having regular DTRs eliminates the question, Is now a good time to bring this up?

And beyond simply creating an environment for discussion, DTRs can and should provide a place for *positive* discourse. A quality conversation is the ultimate goal. We define *quality conversation* as "sympathetic dialogue where two individuals are sharing their experiences, thoughts, feelings, and desires in a friendly, uninterrupted context."[5] A healthy DTR fosters this friendly, uninterrupted context for sharing.

2. A DTR Provides an Outlet for Expression of Needs and Feelings

As the authors of three books on relationships, we've had the opportunity to observe many couples. We've found that the couples with the healthiest relationships are those who talk to each other, not just to others. While it's essential that you have other outlets for your needs and feelings, you need to communicate with the person you're dating.

It's easy to fall into the trap of processing every detail of your relationship with someone outside of it. But that often leads you to think the person you are dating knows the scoop too! A DTR can and should create a space for you two to talk.

3. A DTR Provides an Opportunity to Discover What the Other Person Needs and Feels

A DTR is more than an outlet for your needs and feelings. It's just as much a forum for clarifying and focusing on the needs and feelings of the person you are dating.

A terrific guiding verse for this principle is found in Philippians 2:4. Paul counsels us, "Each of you should look not only to your own interests, but also to the interests of others." We love this verse because of its perfect balance. Paul didn't command that we forget about our own needs altogether. Rather, he said that we should think not *only* of ourselves.

And when it comes to deciding whether you consider your own needs or the needs of others as more important, let Paul's words be your guide: "Do nothing out of selfish ambition or vain conceit, but in humility consider others better than yourselves" (Philippians 2:3). A healthy DTR provides an outlet for your own feelings and creates an environment where you can learn the feelings of another.

This aspect of DTRs makes great practice for marriage. Many times in our own marriage, we've been challenged to *listen* in a conversation when we imagined we'd be doing most of the talking. Particularly in the first few years of our marriage, each of us often assumed that because one of us brought something up or felt deeply about something, that person was the only one who needed to talk. Most of the time, however, the other person had just as much, if not more, to work through and express.

4. A DTR Both Develops and Reveals Character

Our inner nature—or *character*—consists of our values and beliefs. As we learn to consider others better than ourselves, our inner person is built up in strength and beauty. Any conversation in which you are seeking to provide a positive space for dialogue, an outlet for your own feelings, and a means for uncovering what another person needs and feels is going to challenge character development in you and expose the character of the other person.

DTRs develop character because they require us to learn how to communicate, how to balance our needs with those of others, and sometimes how to let go. They also *reveal* character. In her book *Knight in Shining Armor*, P. B. Wilson admonishes us to "remember, when speaking to the opposite sex, the goal is...to uncover the character of someone in whom you might be interested."[6] What better way to see someone's character than to observe how a person responds to the ebb and flow of a relationship? Individuals who respond with flexibility and understanding show good character, while possessive or obsessive people reveal the opposite.

We divulge all kinds of information about our character as we communicate, so an observant person will pay attention to what a DTR indicates about another.

5. A DTR Responds, Rather Than Reacts, to the Progression of a Relationship

At this point, we need to hit on a few things that a DTR is *not* in order to adequately define what it is. A DTR should be not a *reaction* but a *response*. Some people use these terms synonymously, but there is a significant difference between them.

Psychologist and author Gary Rosberg sums it up:

> A *reaction* comes from the gut. It's automatic and at times involuntary. A *response* is thought out and more purposeful. It takes longer to come up with a response, but it's much more effective. As some wise person said, the difference between a reaction and a response is about three seconds.[7]

When we react to a situation, we do so out of immediacy and intensity of feeling. When we respond, however, we have taken the time, however brief, to think things through and to form some kind of judgment based on the facts available to us.

Few things kill relationships faster than consistent reaction. We need to develop the patience to respond and not to react. This patience shows respect for the person with whom we're relating.

We've seen in our relationship that allowing for the space between a reaction and a response slows us down enough to find out what's really going on inside us. It keeps us from the false assumptions that come from gut-level fears and insecurities. If we can stop long enough to respond, we can also more accurately assess what's happening in the relationship.

6. A DTR Should Avoid Destructive Criticism

A DTR is not a time for you to play Holy Spirit. It should not become a forum for you to unload all the things you've observed are wrong with the person you've been dating, even if (*especially* if) that person is in the process of breaking up with you.

Perhaps you genuinely feel that the problems in your relationship are the result of the other person's issues. If that is the case, you need to spend your efforts in prayer first, asking the Holy Spirit—who convicts of sin and speaks into the heart of each believer—to change the other person. Then approach the matter with constructive kindness rather than destructive criticism. Criticism is not the same as expressing your needs and feelings. Criticism attacks the character or actions of another person in order to fix blame and force change. Instead of criticizing the other person, discuss the issues and problems you are facing.

Chances are, the areas you are tempted to criticize are actually the areas you've felt the least able to control or the areas in which you've found yourself most needy and unsatisfied. It's a curious dynamic of criticism that "people tend to criticize...most loudly in the area where they themselves have the deepest emotional need."[8] At this point, criticism is not really about the other person; it's about you. When you are tempted to use a DTR to criticize, take time instead to pray and ask God if you have sought fulfillment in this other person rather than in Him.

7. A DTR Provides a Place for Requests, but Not for Demands

A DTR is the right time to present your requests—the things you hope might change or shape your relationship from this point forward. It is the appropriate time and place to request that the other person meet you halfway. It is *not* the time to demand your way or your "rights." To demand is to insist, to require, to claim as a right. Demands have no place in relationships.

Again, this approach to dating is great training ground for marriage. Within a marriage partnership, you can request that your spouse do or be something, but you can never demand that your spouse change to fit your vision. Think of it this way: "Requests give direction to love, but demands stop the flow of love."[9] A request helps a person know what you need and desire and gives the person guidance in how to meet that need. A demand, on the other hand, puts a person on the defensive and eradicates the possibility for intimacy.

8. Above All, DTRs Should Be Conducted with Love

Love should be the governing principle that shapes all of our interactions with others. Relationships with the opposite sex are no exception.

It may strike you as simplistic or trite to say that DTRs should be conducted with love, but take a look with us at the practical counsel of 1 Corinthians 13, and we think you'll see why it's *essential* that DTRs be handled with love:

> Love is patient, love is kind. It does not envy, it does not boast,
> it is not proud. It is not rude, it is not self-seeking, it is not easily
> angered, it keeps no record of wrongs. Love does not delight in
> evil but rejoices with the truth. (verses 4-6)

Love *is patient*. In other words, it doesn't get ahead of itself. It's easy to rush into a DTR with urgency. It takes patience, however, to develop a healthy relationship.

Love *is kind*. It takes into account the feelings of others. It chooses to say the edifying and encouraging thing rather than the hurtful one. Love respects another person's spirit and treats it with gentleness.

Love *does not envy.* Jealousy is a monster that will consume your relationship if you allow it. Love trusts that what it has is enough. It does not demand more.

Love *does not boast.* It doesn't try to make more of itself. It doesn't use a relationship as an opportunity for bragging. It doesn't strut or puff itself up.

Love *is not proud.* In other words, love is humble. Humility is the choice to elevate the other and diminish yourself. Jesus exemplified humility when He washed the disciples' feet (see John 13:1-17). This was not a glorious, "look at me" job. It was lowly, meek, and wholly loving.

Love *is not rude.* Love watches how it says something. Telling something "like it is," for instance, is not always pure honesty. It can also be a brash or rude act. Manipulating a conversation by not saying anything at all can also be rude. For the stony silent types out there, it may be easier for you to choose to stew rather than communicate. But love is not rude.

Love *is not self-seeking.* Love does not put its own wants and needs first. Love doesn't look for the way it can best be fulfilled. A DTR—a dating relationship on the whole—is not a place to work toward getting your way. Love does not seek its own agenda.

Love *is not easily angered.* Feelings of frustration are bound to arise at some point in a relationship. These emotions can get intense and lead to anger. Love chooses to put anger on hold, listening and seeking to understand first.

Love *keeps no record of wrongs.* Love says no to resentment and bitterness no matter what the outcome of a DTR. Love chooses to believe the best and puts the wrongs done against it out of mind. We all will miscommunicate at some point—that's a guarantee. We need to approach DTRs with the kind of grace that keeps no record of wrongs.

Love *does not delight in evil but rejoices with the truth.* There may come a time when you need to have a DTR because you've gone too far. You want to reclaim the purity of the relationship. Love does not delight in sin, but confesses, repents, and rejoices with holiness. Love enjoys righteousness.[10]

A successful DTR is conducted with healthy communication skills, and healthy communication begins with love. When we see how Scripture describes godly love ("true love"), we are better equipped to define our relationships appropriately and well.

A DTR is a positive, communicative dialogue that provides place and space for a couple to express needs and wants.

Now that we know what a DTR is—and a few things it is not—let's look at when you might use this important relationship tool.

3

When to DTR

We thoroughly enjoyed our dating relationship, but that's not to say it ran without a hitch. In fact, the first time I (Jeramy) called Jerusha was a pretty funny occasion. Now that I've been a part of the Redford family for quite some time, Jerusha and I can laugh about this, but in the heat of the moment, I didn't find the situation quite so amusing.

You see, I didn't know Jerusha well at all. We were both working with the high-school youth group, but the staff and volunteers didn't have much interaction with one another unless they worked with the same class of students. We didn't. I served the seniors at the time, and Jerusha ministered to the sophomores. More than fifty other leaders and five hundred students were around and between us.

Several staff members at the church had counseled (some would say harassed) me to ask Jerusha out. I did my homework and decided I did at least need to meet Jerusha. The next step seemed logical and simple enough: Get Jerusha's phone number and call her up with a date and a plan. Lucky for me (or so I thought), the Redfords were listed in the church directory, so no subterfuge or asking around was necessary.

When I dialed the ten digits, the phone rang a couple of times, and a male voice on the other end said, "Hello."

Now when you picture the ideal way to get in touch with a girl for the first time, it's probably not with an out-of-the-blue phone call to her father. This immediately made me somewhat formal and even a little defensive. Little did I know that things would only get worse!

"Hi. Is Jerusha there?"

Instead of your standard "May I ask who's calling?" or even the disappointing "She's unavailable at the moment," I got hit with…

"How did you get this number?"

What I didn't know was that the church directory listed only one of the two numbers for the Redford home. That number just happened to be the line Jerusha's dad had recently transferred for use in his home office. It was not supposed to be used for "personal calls" like this one.

This was not at all how I had planned the phone call to go. It seemed as if Jerusha's dad was asking for my intentions with her before I'd even talked to her! But therein lies the irony of the situation. It made me ask myself exactly what I was doing with Jerusha's number. Jerusha and I joke around that we had to have a DTR before most people do simply to make it safe for me to call the house. And that phone call probably happened so we could share the humor and the discomfort with you right now!

That was certainly a defining moment for our relationship, one that we still enjoy laughing about as a family. Lucky for me, Jerusha's dad decided to give me their home number and let Jerusha take things from there. This "problem" was easily resolved. But as we began to date, we reached many other points that caused us to consider our relationship and its progress. These defining moments led us to DTRs that helped shape our relationship and guide it through both the glitches and the still waters.

DEFINING MOMENTS

After we had been talking and hanging out together for a couple of weeks, Jeramy came over to see me (Jerusha) at my house. I'd been asked to speak at youth group the next night—sort of spur of the moment—and wanted to study, but I also wanted to see Jeramy. I asked if he wanted to come over so we could see each other for a few minutes in between my reading and writing.

This was another defining point in our relationship. When Jeramy showed up, I was in an intense, scholarly kind of mood. The tone was serious, and the house was dead quiet. It turned out to be an awkward, heavy hour. When Jeramy got up to go, I walked him to the door. We didn't know what to do, so we shook hands and said good-bye. It was weird and stiff.

No sooner had the door closed than my mom came up behind me and said, "You guys are way too wooden about all this. You need to relax." We wanted to date the "right" way, but we were too uptight, totally unable to be ourselves.

Jeramy called a few minutes after he got home to ask if there was something wrong. I confessed that I thought he would be impressed if I seemed serious about studying God's Word. Jeramy was then able to admit that he was a bit overwhelmed by some of the things I said. My airs and collegiate vocabulary didn't fit with the get-to-know-you vibe of a date.

We were able to have a brief conversation to clear the air and, importantly, to define our relationship as one that wasn't going to be about impressing each other or even about figuring each other out. Saying what we were thinking helped the atmosphere and allowed us to move on.

Also near the beginning of our relationship, we used DTR to establish that we were interested in each other and on the same level. This took some of the pressure off our relationship because we weren't constantly wondering if every phone call "meant" something.

These initial stages were full of anticipation, excitement, and a healthy dose of uncertainty. After all, the DTRs that start a relationship don't set anything in stone. We had begun with some good communication, but it takes more than one or two conversations to make a healthy relationship.

One Wednesday night after high-school ministry, we decided to talk for a while. At this point we'd gone on some great dates and spent quite a bit of time conversing on the phone and hanging out in different situations. We'd also had those initial DTRs, but this night provided the opportunity for us to discuss our relationship further and determine that we would date exclusively. We also talked through our physical and emotional standards of purity. Once again this open communication was a freeing thing, removing tension from our dates and conversations. All it took was a willingness to speak with honesty and sensitivity and a little effort toward that end.

Some time later we were established as a couple in the eyes of others, including our families and friends. We started being invited to and attending social events together. During the wedding reception of some mutual friends, I (Jerusha) was shocked to see Jeramy break dancing in the middle of a circle of clapping guests. Though we had defined our relationship well, there were still plenty of natural and fun surprises in our interactions.

We also attended family celebrations together, including a housewarming party for Jerusha's sister and her husband. This night proved to be another defining moment for us as a couple. One of the guys Jerusha had been interested in during college was still friends with her sister and had been invited to the party. Jerusha mentioned this casually to Jeramy, and it raised a few questions in his mind: *Why would she bring up someone from her past? Did this negate anything we had determined or discussed?*

We had a great time at the party, and this guy never made an appearance. But the possibility precipitated a good talk about how serious we were about each other. It provided us an opportunity to redefine our relationship and strengthen it further.

As we discovered more about each other, issues came up that needed explanation. The longer you talk to someone, the more you need of that person's story to determine if you'll move forward with the relationship. That's part of the natural progression of two people getting to know each other, and learning more about each other triggered further defining moments in our relationship.

Ultimately, there came a time when the proverbial handwriting was on the wall. The defining moments that began and shaped our relationship had led to a crossroads for the ultimate decision—marry or break up.

Our families both supported our relationship. In fact, a funny defining moment for Jeramy occurred when Jerusha's then eleven-year-old brother lured him to the computer desk, presumably to show him his new game.

It was one of those design-your-own maze and message programs, and Ian had created an intricate series of planes flying into balloons, popping them to reveal one letter at a time. After a minute the message was clear: "Marry Rusha," the computer screen proclaimed.

The process of dating and relating had narrowed our options to two: marry or break up. There was little need now for DTR-type conversations to reveal what we thought about each other.

But a couple of additional defining moments nevertheless shaped our future. One of the most significant came through Doug, a mentor and fellow minister of Jeramy's. Jeramy was sitting with Doug in a diner when Doug challenged him, "So what are you waiting for?" Jeramy decided that the answer was "Nothing." He left planning the proposal.

Jeramy arranged for one more DTR the day he proposed to Jerusha. While looking out over the Catalina harbor, he told Jerusha how he defined love. He confessed that he wanted to spend the rest of his life loving her, and then he got down on one knee to see if she felt the same. She did—and then some!

A chronicle of defining moments ended for us in engagement. As we paused during the different stages of our relationship to define what was happening and where things were headed, we enjoyed the freedom and peace the discussions brought to our courtship.

When to DTR will be slightly different for each couple. Yet in the natural progression of a relationship, defining moments will provide you the opportunity to assess, evaluate, and guide your interaction with each other.

PRECIPITATING FACTORS

In later chapters we'll look at different stages of a relationship and the various times within each stage that you may wonder what prompts a DTR and when and how to make it happen. In this chapter we want to provide you with some *general* guidelines for when to DTR.

As you can see from our own story, defining moments arise that provide for and sometimes *require* DTRs. Precipitating factors will often nudge a couple in the direction of a DTR—and occasionally plunge them headlong into one! Though we cannot create an exhaustive list of every possible "defining moment," we've come up with some common ones. As you progress through your relationship, keep in mind that the following nine situations are good times for a DTR.

1. You Need Boundaries

Setting physical and emotional limits for your relationship protects you from becoming too intimate too quickly. If you've been in a relationship for any length of time and not yet discussed these important issues, you'd benefit from having a DTR to establish your standards as a couple. We will have much more to say about this topic later in the book, but for now know that if guidelines have not been set, it's time to DTR.

2. Something Is New

It's often easiest for people (especially sensitive ones) to bring things up in a sideways or backdoor way. Instead of initiating a conversation about where a relationship might be headed, for instance, someone might hint that his lease will be up in three months and he needs to decide how long to renew it for. Or a woman might mention casually that she's gotten back in touch with a former boyfriend, leaving her current boyfriend to question whether she is pulling back from the relationship or may be unsure of *his* feelings. If you notice that the person you're dating is hinting at or mentioning things that you haven't discussed together, this is a good time for a DTR.

3. You're Concerned

You're not happy with the way things are going. Something may have happened, or the tensions and pressures of day-to-day relating may simply have worn down the relationship. Maybe you've had a big fight or something's bugging you. In any case, it's time for a "refreshment DTR," a conversation to determine whether the health and joy of your relationship can be reestablished. At this time you may need to discuss further emotional and physical boundaries or set guidelines for other aspects of your relationship. Whatever the unique situation, if you find yourself dissatisfied with how things are going, it's time to assess and evaluate using the DTR tool.

4. Things Have Changed

In other words, things aren't "normal" anymore. You may not exactly be displeased with the direction the relationship is headed, but something seems different. You can sense that things have changed, and you're not certain why or how. It could be that the other person is dissatisfied. It may be that you don't get the regular phone call you've come to expect. Or perhaps you've begun to question where you stand because the dynamic of your relationship has changed. Maybe *nothing* is amiss. For instance, if a guy is silent, it may not *mean* anything. (Perhaps his silence simply proves what Jerry Seinfeld joked, "Do you want to know what men are thinkin'?... Nothin'!") Yet when you begin to sense that things aren't as they have been or as they "should" be, chances are good it's time for a DTR.

5. An Awkward Moment

As we mentioned, at certain times, particularly at the front end of our relationship, things just didn't flow smoothly. Clarifying things after a confusing interaction doesn't require a huge, drawn-out, "But how do you *feel?*" kind of DTR. Yet a brief conversation to acknowledge the awkwardness and move beyond it can do much for the health of a relationship. Besides, if you allow too many uncomfortable times to go unchecked, you may find your relationship weighed down unnecessarily.

6. A Key Event

This may sound silly, but what happens when you go to a wedding and the girl you're dating catches the bouquet? Well, nothing technically, but you may feel put on the spot. And what about when she graduates or he is offered a new job and questions about the future loom? Can a special Valentine's Day date or anniversary define your relationship without you knowing it? Absolutely. Certain events carry an inherent weight for relationships. In order to stay in touch with where the other person is and what he is thinking, you need to observe the person you're dating as well as remain in touch with where you are.

7. Someone Moves

This key event is worth mentioning specifically because, while some events do not require a DTR, a move *always* necessitates a defining or redefining conversation. A DTR at this juncture includes questions such as, Will we continue to date? If so, how seriously and how exclusively? Will we be able to see each other? How often? Will we be able to afford telephone calls and gas/mileage for visits? A move is a huge defining moment for any relationship, and a DTR should address the practical aspects of the transition.

8. Others Make Comments

How often we've watched couples squirm under the eagle eyes and crafty commentary of well-meaning friends and family! It can be incredibly difficult to stay on the same page with someone when others are making remarks like "Well, I guess you'll be the next one down the aisle" or asking questions such as "You've been together *how* long?" No matter where you are in life, you will run into people who will cause you to doubt how you've defined your relationship. Be as aware as you can of what's being said to the person you're with. If the questions or comments seem to be affecting one or both of you, suggest a DTR before things get out of hand.

9. You Cross Physical Boundaries

If you have stepped over the line as a couple, you most likely need to have a conversation to reestablish your commitment to purity. Confess your failings to God (in other words, agree with Him that what you did was wrong) and then to each other. Pray as a couple the words David prayed in Psalm 51: "Create in me a pure heart, O God, and renew a steadfast spirit within me.... Restore to me the joy of your salvation and grant me a willing spirit, to sustain me" (verses 10,12). Also use this DTR to plan how you might avoid compromising your standards again.

This list of defining moments is not exhaustive, but it includes moments that may help you shape your relationship. Simply being aware of these precipitating factors can help you know when to DTR.

FUNDAMENTALS

Now we want to offer some additional, pragmatic how-tos, which we hope will help you successfully determine when to DTR.

First, you must **set aside a time.** This may sound obvious, but too often people try to squeeze a DTR in between things—on the way to the movies, just as they're saying good-night after a date, or when they have to be at church in five minutes. Maybe they're having dinner with another couple at seven, and at quarter of seven they decide they're going to try to talk about their feelings and needs *right then.* Yeah, right!

DTRs often take longer than you anticipate, and most likely you'll find yourself rushing to finish if you've planned things too closely together. You need to plan a time and give yourself plenty of wiggle room.

Remember, DTR equals communication. And "communication is a process that allows two…people in a relationship to express their hearts to each other. It not only entails expression, but also a commitment to listening and understanding.… To do this effectively we need to…plan a time and setting for it to take place."[1] Don't simply go with the flow. Set aside a time. Communicating, listening, and understanding will take more than five minutes.

Second, you should weigh **day versus night.** For some reason, feelings and emotions get heightened the later at night it gets, and we're often freer with our words and feelings as our bodies wind down. While there's no hard and fast rule that DTRs should happen during daylight hours, we *do* recommend that you plan to talk earlier rather than later in the day if at all possible. If that won't work for your schedule, think about the difference between seven in the evening and two o'clock in the morning. If you are already setting aside a time to DTR, it shouldn't be too difficult to plan it at time when you'll be less likely to fall into extreme emotionality.

You should also think about whether to DTR **in public versus in private.** Do you remember our friend Andrea from chapter 2? On her college campus it was an unspoken rule that DTRs happen in semiprivate public places. She explained that a couple is much less likely to get into a knockdown-drag-out fight in a public place or to cry too dramatically if others are close by. People are also less prone to end up making out after getting so excited about what they determine about their relationship. We'd call this commonsense wisdom. You need to have enough privacy to talk openly and intimately, but you should also protect yourself from the pitfalls of too private a time and locale.

In addition, it's best to DTR **after seeking counsel.** We always recommend that each partner in a couple be mentored by someone older in the Christian faith, and when you're considering a DTR, it's important to take a minute to solicit that mentor's godly counsel. This *doesn't* mean asking every single one of your friends for advice, and it certainly doesn't encourage you to gossip. It simply calls you to use a trusted and godly person as a sounding board for the thoughts and feelings you plan to express in a DTR. Proverbs 15:22 declares, "Plans fail for lack of counsel." Seeking outside assistance will help a DTR succeed.

Even more important, you should DTR only **after you talk it over with God.** Prayer is not an afterthought to a DTR. Colossians 4:2 calls believers to "devote yourselves to prayer." That command means committing each step of your relationship to prayer with fervor and consistency. But you should also set aside a *specific* time for prayer before a DTR—a time to ask the Lord for wisdom, guidance, peace, balance… You name it, you may need it! Prayer before a DTR will guard your mind in Christ

Jesus and help keep your focus on eternity rather than only on the moment at hand (see Philippians 4:7).

Now just as there are times when you *should* DTR, there are also times when you should *not*. Let us give you these three "nots" to round out our list.

1. Not After a Romantic Date

After a great date together, might you be too caught up in emotions to communicate effectively? Sure. Anybody would be. But, you may ask, couldn't a romantic date be a "defining moment" or a "key event" like the ones described earlier? Definitely. But *immediately* after you spend this time together is *not* the moment to launch into a DTR. Give yourself some space—a day, some hours at the very least. Let yourself come down to a more objective place. Think of it this way: You *still* need to set aside a time, receive counsel, and pray! That'll cool you down enough to think levelheadedly in preparation for your DTR.

2. Not After a Big Fight

Everything looks worse after a huge blowup. The frustrations caused by a fight or even by simple annoyances can drastically affect the nature and course of a DTR. Once again, you need to cool down and come to a more realistic and balanced state of mind. People don't call for an appraisal of their home after a hurricane or fire. They wait for things to get back to "normal" before estimating what their house is worth. Give yourself some space after a big fight. Your feelings may or may not change, but your ability to speak with kindness and patience will change significantly.

3. Not Before It's Time

This is by far the most difficult concept for people to grab hold of. But keep in mind that it's very easy to talk or worry a relationship to death. A preemptive strike might even destroy a friendship that could develop into a dating relationship given appropriate time and space. For instance, driving home from that awkward scholarly time at Jerusha's, I (Jeramy) began jumping to conclusions about our chemistry. This could have led me to a serious DTR before it was time, and now I can see that a premature DTR would have been a big mistake. Jerusha and I needed to discuss what happened that evening, but it was too soon to discuss the overall direction of our relationship. The conversation would have come out of fear and insecurity rather than wisdom and patience.

It takes balance and restraint to know when it *is* time for a DTR. We all want to know where we stand with people. We long to have things clearly defined at every moment. But DTRs cannot eliminate all the messiness of relationships. A DTR is a tool that can help you avoid some of the pitfalls and mysteries of relating to the opposite sex, but like any other tool, it has limitations. This is why judgment and discernment are crucial. Learn to decide when and when *not* to DTR by seeking the Lord, who gives wisdom and understanding. As God declares in Proverbs 3, "Preserve sound judgment and discernment, do not let them out of your sight; they will be life for you, an ornament to grace your neck. Then you will go on your way in safety, and your foot will not stumble.... For the LORD will be your confidence" (verses 21-23,26). Pray for the Lord's discernment and you will know when and when not to DTR.

IN REAL LIFE

To close the chapter, we want to share with you a story that illustrates why *not* to DTR before it's time. We know that it's a great challenge to determine when to DTR and when to wait. We think this story will help you see that at times it is very appropriate to hold off.

Mark rock climbs a couple of times a week, usually at the same gym in town. He's been climbing there since it opened and has great relationships with the staff and his fellow climbers.

A few months ago a woman started coming to the gym every Tuesday. She and Mark often ran into each other and exchanged friendly words. She seemed like a nice person, and Mark was impressed by her skill on the wall.

After meeting in passing several times, the woman stopped Mark one evening on his way out. She asked if he'd mind belaying her for one last climb. "My partner had to head home, but I really want to get one more in," she said.

Mark agreed and suggested that if he was going to take responsibility for her safety, he probably should know her name. He introduced himself first and told her that she could call him by his superhero name, "The Belay-er." She laughed and shook his hand. "I'm Kim. Not Kimberly. Just Kim."

Mark prepared to belay and called, "Okay, 'Just Kim,' climb on." Mark watched as she deftly scaled the most difficult wall in the gym. Again, he was struck by her athletic abilities.

As she rappelled down, Mark steadied the ropes. She hit the rocky bed triumphantly. "Thanks," she said, releasing her harness and removing her helmet. "I really needed that."

Mark made a mock bow and told her he was glad to be of service. She giggled and declared him the most chivalrous partner she'd had in quite some time. He thanked her, made sure she didn't need any help wrapping the ropes, and headed out.

Mark didn't think twice about his short interaction with Kim, but when he walked into the gym the following Tuesday, Kim revealed that she had. "Hey, Mark! I enjoyed climbing with you last week. Maybe you and I could get together sometime."

Mark didn't know what to say. It seemed that she was asking him out.

But *no*. She probably just thought it was cool to climb with someone different. Not wanting to extend his awkward pause any longer, he blurted out, "Sure. Yeah. That'd be great."

"How about Saturday? I thought maybe we could hit one of the trails around the national forest."

Mark paused again. *Okay. Maybe she is asking me out. What do I do? I'm not really attracted to her. Will I hurt her feelings if I say no? Will I be leading her on if I say yes? Wait! What in the world am I thinking? The girl wants to hike with me, not have dinner. It'll probably be fun.*

"What time?" Mark asked.

They headed out on Saturday around 10 a.m. When they crested the top of a canyon in the forest's center, they saw gorgeous skies serving as a backdrop to a breathtaking view of the mountains. Mark stretched out his arms and took a deep breath. The two-hour hike had been a blast. He and Kim had talked about everything from career to the cosmos. He'd discovered that she was a believer and attended what he knew to be a strong, Bible-believing church on the outskirts of town.

They'd really clicked. And things had been so low-key. He was glad that he hadn't freaked out and assumed that Kim wanted more than just a friendship. When she pulled out a sack lunch for the two of them that was better than anything he'd cooked for himself in a month, he felt even more pleased.

After reaching the trail head a couple of hours later, they both said what a good time they'd had. As Kim stepped into her car and turned the ignition, she called over the roar, "See ya Tuesday."

He did see her Tuesday, but he had brought Darren, one of his buddies from work, to climb with him, and he didn't even catch Kim's eye during the two-hour climbing session. When Darren headed for the shower, Mark passed by the wall where Kim had climbed and waved to her as she rolled ropes.

As he turned his back to walk away, he could feel her staring at him. "Is that it, Mark?"

"What?"

"All you're gonna do is wave? We go out, have a great time, and all you do is *wave?* I just need to know where we stand."

Dumbfounded, Mark stammered again, "What?" He felt sick. Confused. "I don't know what you mean, Kim," he managed to get out.

She looked at him with wounded eyes. "Never mind. I see how it is." Mark tried to reply, but she spun on her heels and walked away.

Mark didn't know how to react. Part of him wanted to run after her and apologize. He had no idea she had invested so much in their time together. The other part of him wanted to run as far away from Kim as possible.

Mark told Darren good-bye and drove home. After taking a Gatorade from the fridge, he sat down on the chair next to his answering machine. "You have one new message," the computerized voice droned. "First message…"

"Hey, Mark, this is Kim. Don't freak. Jay from the gym gave me your number so I could apologize. I made such a fool of myself. I was *way* too aggressive. I totally understand your confusion, and I just want to say that all I want is to be friends. I hope you're still interested in that. No pressure. I have fun with you. I think we could be…"

The machine cut her off. Mark didn't feel like drinking the rest of his Gatorade.

With Mark's story in mind, you might want to consider other times when it would be right to wait on a DTR. But let's get right back to stories of when *to* DTR. The next three chapters will focus on DTRs at the beginning, middle, and end of a relationship.

4

In the Beginning

The start of a relationship can be full of surprises. You can't predict what will happen when you interact with another person. Relationships between flawed humans (and that means *any* human) can definitely be messy! But you can and should prepare yourself for a healthy relationship by *planning* to start well.

Laying a foundation for a relationship that's healthy and honoring to the Lord will save you from a situation like the one in which our friend Vickie found herself.

Vickie went to school in another state, so when she returned home for the summer, we were interested in catching up. Over coffee, we told her we planned to write a book on defining relationships, and she groaned. Obviously, she had a story to tell.

Vickie met Steve in one of her classes. They quickly became friends and study partners, and they also had several mutual acquaintances. They started spending a lot of time together, and before long people were making comments and assuming the two were a couple. Vickie was interested in Steve, and she thought it safe to assume he felt the same. Why else would he invest so much time in her?

Vickie shared more of her heart with Steve than she had with any other guy. They talked so easily. But Steve didn't open up about himself much unless Vickie asked specific questions. She didn't really worry about this, assuming that most guys are reluctant to talk on a more personal level. Meanwhile, Vickie became more and more attached to Steve.

Finally, Steve asked her out for a date. Vickie was sure "this was it." He arranged to pick her up at her room at seven o'clock on Saturday night.

The "date" turned out to be a disappointment. Steve didn't have a plan of any sort, and they ended up at the same cheap Mexican diner they always went to with their group. Since Steve "didn't feel like going home yet," they wandered around town looking in closed shop windows and finally ended up at the movies.

Vickie had anticipated something special, but Steve didn't even treat. It was as if they were two buddies hanging out for the night. By the time they got back to her room, all Vickie wanted to do was curl up with a good book for a few minutes before she fell asleep.

When Steve walked her to the door, however, he bent forward and kissed her. Vickie was so shocked she didn't have time to stop him, nor did she really want to. In that instant, she forgot all her disappointment. Her mind spun: *He really does care… A kiss means something.*

Over the next few days, Vickie alternated between feeling as if she could conquer the world and feeling as if she were dying inside. She tried to figure out what Steve's every comment meant, but she *was not* going to ask him. *The man should lead the relationship,* she thought. *He should tell me what he's thinking.*

Finally, two weeks later, she broke down and confronted Steve. By this point she was so exasperated that all she could come up with was "Steve, what is up with us?" His dumbfounded look broke her heart and made her angry all in the same minute.

"Well, we're friends, right?"

"Yes," she stammered, trying to keep her composure.

"So that's cool."

Oh my, Vickie thought. *Not only does this guy not care about me, but he's also about as articulate as a farm pig.*

"And that's it?" Vickie showed her frustration for the first time.

"Yeah. You know, I'm just not ready for anything else."

Vickie ended the conversation as quickly as she could and went home raging, crying, totally undone.

We empathized with Vickie, one of the sweetest, most genuine girls we know. She hadn't started the relationship well. She hadn't clarified intentions despite the fact that as time went on she became emotionally attached to Steve. And then a physical display of affection confused her further.

Had Vickie tried to define the relationship earlier and set some boundaries, she probably would have saved herself some heartbreak and frustration. Though starting a relationship well doesn't guarantee that things will end in a happily-ever-after way, it *will* eliminate a great number of problems that can arise in the course of interacting with someone of the opposite sex.

So let's look at where a healthy relationship starts (the answer may surprise you), what role interest and attraction play in the beginning, and how to navigate a first date, a second date, and the important initial DTR.

WHERE IT ALL STARTS

Before a relationship begins—and after it ends—there is one common factor: *you.* Though you can and will be changed by the influence of another person, you will stay *you.* So the secret to success in beginning any relationship well is to start with you. It's crucial that you establish a clear picture of who you are and what you're looking for in a person of the opposite sex.[1] And before you think about the practical details of starting the dating process, it's important to think about the key elements to building your *own* strong foundation.

First you must **determine what you've *been* looking for**. During your years of relating to others, certain hopes and expectations for a member of the opposite sex have grown in your heart. Take some time to evaluate those. Think through which ones are negotiable and which ones are not. Consider making a list of those desires and praying through them. Ask the Lord for guidance and then seek the counsel of someone who knows you and knows the Lord.

Next take any steps necessary to **transition into what you *should be* looking for**. If your list of expectations has missed the mark, take some time to reorder your thinking. Read books about character and what it takes to become a godly person. Search the Scriptures for descriptions of men and women of character; those will reveal to you what God would have you pursue in a relationship. (We've included an entire chapter of biblical models near the end of this book; that may be a good place for you to start.) And as you continue to look to God for clear direction, you'll be able to conform what you've been pursuing to what He would have you seek.

The next phase includes **making an honest assessment of your current stage of life** and determining what you might be ready for in a relationship. If you know that you're going to spend the next few years in rigorous study or a career internship, you'll want to weigh the feelings and needs of the other person before you start a relationship. If, on the other hand, you believe you're ready for a deeper commitment, you'll want to steer clear of the kind of casual relationships that others might be looking to enter.

The final key is to take into account your past relationships—what has been healthy and what has been unhealthy. This means you need to **grow from the past**. If you become jealous easily, for instance, you may want to work at getting to the root of that issue before you consider diving into a relationship. If physical purity has been an area of struggle for you, it's time to dissect the causes and effects of that sin.

A good friend of ours tried to bypass this last step, and she moved directly from a relationship in which she had been too physically intimate to another relationship. She felt confident that things would be different simply because she was with a different guy. It was no surprise that she found herself going down the same path—too far too quickly and feeling desperate for things to change.

What this woman failed to do was to take a break from relationships and to grow from her past. She needed to learn from her mistakes, allow for healing, and then work on changing. Instead, she entered the second relationship at a "–1." No matter how hard you try, the best you can get when adding one to a negative one is zero. It's simple arithmetic. And it's why we caution people to avoid the "rebound."

Growing from the past is probably the most important factor in starting things well in a new relationship. Being realistic with where you've been and where you hope to be allows you to change and be shaped by the experience of your past.

So before someone else even enters the picture, deal with *you!* Once you've dealt with you, you'll have room to deal with others. It's unrealistic to think you won't notice others while you're working on yourself, and we also realize you might have to exercise self-discipline in order to put off becoming involved with someone before you're ready. But we guarantee that postponing the next relationship for these reasons will be worth it.

THE OTHER

In order to understand how to start things well, we've got to go back to the very beginning of any relationship. A person enters your world. Your radar picks up something new and different. You have got to figure out what's going on.

Your initial contact with someone can elicit any feeling from a mundane *Oh, someone new is in my writers' group* to the rush of *I can't believe how attracted I am to that person.*

As you know, lots of relationships do not begin with the overtone of romance. Many first contacts with the opposite sex simply develop into friendship, and friendship is a great starting point for a relationship because it allows you to get to know someone without the clutter of romantic emotions. If a friendship morphs into a romantic relationship, you probably knew enough about the person to determine that she was worth pursuing romantically.

When you become interested in someone totally new to your world, however, the best thing to do first is educate yourself. Find out what you can about this person before going any further. Gather all the information you can and then decide if this person is worth pursuing. Whether you start as friends or with immediate romantic interest and attraction, learning what you can about a person before you move forward will help you start a relationship well. You can learn about a person by asking around, observing him in a variety of situations, and watching closely how he handles joys, challenges, and obligations.

People are usually drawn to each other for several reasons. Physical attraction is usually the first, the most common, and the most difficult reason to objectively evaluate. A shallow interest based on looks can develop into a healthy attraction. If your attraction begins and ends with a person's physical appearance, though, you're not establishing the right kind of foundation for a healthy dating relationship.

You may also find yourself attracted to someone because you connect with her on common enjoyments and experiences. You both like to camp, and you both get a thrill from talking about the upcoming sale at the downtown sporting goods store. You both chose the liberal arts track at a science and engineering school, and you can help and support each other. You both walk your dogs at the same time before work. The list of possible connecting points is endless.

You may also find yourself attracted to someone's mind and spirit. You share ideas with a person, and he "gets" what you're saying. You're drawn to the way someone expresses herself in a Bible study. You're attracted by the character qualities or virtues someone models.

You will want to marry someone whom you are attracted to on many different levels. But during the first stages of dating, you may find that you're drawn to one aspect of a person in particular. Later, other facets of that person's personality may even be a turnoff! Casually dating, rather than jumping into a more serious relationship, will help you to narrow your options down to those of the opposite sex who will best complement you. Some of the people you date will remain your friends, some you may date a couple of times, and some you will invest a longer period of time in getting to know.

All relationships start with some level of *interest* and *attraction*. The next step to beginning things well is to find out what you can about that person and determine whether you'd like to be friends or develop something more. For many, the natural progression of interest and attraction will lead to a first date.

First Date

Defining a relationship well from the get-go involves thinking through all the details of a first date. You're probably already familiar with the basics, but it can be helpful to look at them again.

For example, be specific when you ask someone out. Don't try the nebulous approach of "Would you like to go out sometime?" Ask instead for a specific date and time. Ask a week to ten days in advance to allow someone sufficient time to plan. It's also good to offer options for the date and to be willing to modify your plans. (When Jeramy showed up at Jerusha's house for their first date, he told her parents that he planned to take her to a nearby Chinese restaurant. When they exchanged sidelong glances, Jeramy figured out that Chinese *wouldn't* be the way to go! He put Plan B into action. It turned out to be a much more successful first date as a result.) It's also important to remember that an invitation means an offer to pay. If you can't afford to take someone out on your own, get to know that person in a group context instead.

Once you've gotten beyond asking for a date, you'll need to arrange the details. As you design a first date, plan something you both can enjoy. It's no good trying to seem "cultured" and suggest attending the opera if both of you will be bored out of your minds. Be who you are and choose something you'll have fun doing. It's also smart to choose a date in a familiar area so you aren't lost or flustered. You'll also want to know how much the date will cost you and make plans that work with your budget. Also, keep in mind any time restraints your date might have. Wear a watch and respectfully gauge whether your date seems ready to go home early.

One of the most important things to remember is that a first date is the time to begin to get to know someone. Go somewhere where you can *talk*. If you choose a location where conversation is difficult or impossible, you won't be able to find out anything about your date.

Remember, a first date doesn't have to resolve whether a person is marriage material or even whether you want to start an official relationship. Simply getting to know a person well enough to determine if you'd enjoy a second date is a good goal for Date 1. The only way to do this is to be honest with yourself and with your date. Don't try to please or impress this person with falsehoods, hoping to get him to like you enough to take you out again. You don't need to tell lies in order to interest someone enough for a second date.

Round Two

A second date continues the process of getting to know someone. We've noticed that it's easy to make speedy assumptions this early in a relationship. The way your date says something tweaks you, for instance, and you wonder what that indicates about her character or your future together. Or your date doesn't seem interested, so you figure you'll step back to avoid getting hurt. Assumptions may preclude the choice of going on a second date altogether. But if you opt for a second date, keep your eyes open and try to determine whether your assumptions seem to be affirmed by the other person's behavior.

We've also observed that many people place a lot of weight on a second date. All of a sudden they think they need to define their intentions and their boundaries. In most instances, a second date is not the time for a DTR. A second date is a next step, not necessarily a relationship. A second date is a chance to reveal a bit more about yourself, but it's not a time for confessionals and spilling your guts. And a second date is a time for conversation, not displays of affection. A second date should remain casual with as little pressure as possible. It's a time to determine whether you're interested enough to continue seeing a person.

And Beyond

When a couple's been on a few dates, their relationship could go one of several ways. If a twosome finds they connect on a deep level, their interaction may quickly transition into a dating relationship. This necessitates a DTR conversation early on, perhaps even after the second date.

Other couples may continue to date on a casual level for another couple of weeks or more before a DTR becomes necessary.

Some people who've known each other for a while begin a relationship without going on dates at all. They start to date after they've decided to pursue each other. They may have a DTR before their first date.

All of these factors make it impossible to say exactly when you should have a DTR to set the tone and pace of a relationship. The specific time will be unique to each couple. And the beginning of a relationship will always include a certain level of mystery and the unknown. Yes, that can be frustrating, but trying to force a quick DTR will not eliminate all the questions about a relationship's potential and future.

This is one reason why it's essential to know yourself and to be comfortable with yourself in the Lord—completely distinct from another person. If you continually spend time defining that most important relationship, you'll be able to weather the beginning stages of every other relationship. Looking for a relationship to satisfy a deeper need than it can provide will leave you aggravated by the inevitable indefinites of a new relationship.

We would suggest that if you've seen and talked to a person for a month and haven't had a DTR, it's probably a good idea to do so. We use this one-month guideline loosely, though, since some relationships will need a DTR sooner.

The most important thing to do is exercise wisdom and discernment in your particular situation. You don't want to jump the gun like Kim from the rock-climbing gym. Yet you also don't want to leave yourself or your date hanging in confusion. You will be better able to determine a good time to DTR if you are aware of your own feelings and the other person's signals.

As a note, until you have had a DTR, we think it best to avoid physical affection. Besides showing respect for the other person, this practice will keep the initial stages of your dating casual and free of the unnecessary confusion that undefined touching often brings. As we will explore in the next section, in a DTR you will establish your physical boundaries. Until you have that limitation clarified, you don't know what will and will not cause the other person to stumble.

A Personal DTR

Once you've determined it's time for a DTR, you should assess some things privately before you approach the person you've been seeing. This will be sort of a personal DTR, a time for you to think through how *you'd* like to define the relationship.

During this time consider, *Is this a person I want to continue to pursue or by whom I'd like to be pursued?* If the answer is no, now is the time to bow out. Don't hold on to a young relationship because you're hoping that things might change, a spark might ignite, or you like having something to do on a Saturday night. Be realistic about your own feelings so you can show respect and honor for the other person.

I (Jerusha) wish I'd taken time for personal DTRs in my college dating relationships. I didn't stop to evaluate my own intentions seriously, and by the time a DTR came around, the guy wanted to become exclusive, when I was thinking it was just nice to have a date every weekend. I regret not taking the time to honestly assess my own feelings.

If you decide you would like to continue getting to know this person, take a few moments to answer the following questions:

- What do I hope this relationship will become?
- Where do I hope this relationship will be in six months?
- Do I have any expectations for this relationship? Are these healthy or not?
- What are appropriate physical and emotional boundaries for us?
- How does this person fit (or not fit) with what I'm looking for long-term?
- Does this person have a genuine faith in Christ, one that will encourage mine?

The purpose of this personal DTR is not to answer all of these questions definitively, but to help you determine what you're thinking and feeling about the relationship. You will return to these questions again and again if the relationship continues to progress. And you may find your answers changing in response to how the other person feels.

At this point you might want to journal some of your thoughts and then revisit them when you're a month, two months, or even further into the relationship.

The Defined Unknown

Now that you've established a personal definition of your relationship, you're ready to talk to the other person. When you set up a time for a DTR, let the person know that you'd like to talk about where your relationship is headed. This will give her the opportunity to have a personal DTR time as well. If you spring a DTR on someone out of the blue, she may not have processed her thoughts and may be unable to articulate where she sees things headed.

The time will come when you sit down to talk. There are three categories of information to cover within a DTR at the beginning of a relationship. The first is *interest;* the second is *intentions;* and the third is *boundaries.* We recommend you cover these three elements in order.

Start by establishing whether both parties share the same level of interest. You will be taking a risk in initiating a DTR because you will be voicing your own feelings first. If you are interested in pursuing an exclusive dating relationship, express that desire. If you want to continue on a casual level, communicate that you are interested in the other person but not ready for a commitment to exclusivity. Then your date has a chance to respond and voice his level of interest. If he does not share the same opinion, you can choose to end things or discuss how to reconcile your differences.

Needless to say, if one person wants to continue in a relationship and the other doesn't, you're not going to be moving on to the intentions phase of the DTR. If the other person has decided that it's time to stop seeing you, things should end. This may be hard, especially if during your personal DTR you pictured what Christmas gift you were going to buy her. But it's important to be willing to let go.

You can try to compromise if one person wants to stay casual and the other would like to be serious. The key is to be completely honest with each other. It does no good to try to shield the feelings of another by pretending you are more interested than you are. Likewise, it harms rather than benefits your relationship to act as if you are satisfied with whatever level of interest he expresses.

Best-case scenario: Your levels of interest match as closely as possible. You both sense that your relationship is headed in a specific direction, and you want to explore the potential together.

Next, clarify your intentions. We define intentions (with good ol' *Webster's* help) as "purpose or attitude toward the effect of one's actions or conduct." Intentions are not the same as promises, and it's important that both of you understand that expressing the *intention* to see each other weekly or call every so often is not the same as committing a person to some sort of rigid schedule.

Clarifying your intentions simply means agreeing upon a purposeful way to conduct your relationship. Discuss what strategy you will employ to nurture and develop your relationship. Are you a "look ahead" couple who will set dates far in advance or spontaneous types who will wing it week to week? What title will you give to the relationship and how will you speak of it to others? What will you do to balance the relationship with other areas of your life—work, studies, friendships, family, hobbies?

This discussion of intentions will naturally lead you to the final subject of an initial DTR—boundaries. Together, you will need to establish specific physical and emotional boundaries for your relationship.[2]

Later in the book, we'll look more specifically at how couples can talk about physical and emotional issues, but for now we will encourage you with these words: Boundaries help you maintain appropriate levels of intimacy in your dating relationship. They allow you to freely get to know a person, and they protect you from becoming too close too soon.

Some Christians have considered their personal physical boundaries and determined what they will and will not do before marriage. Bringing your convictions before another person takes courage and maturity, but think how honored the Lord will be when you share with the person you are dating what He's laid upon your heart.

A physical boundary should be clearly defined from the beginning of a relationship. Vague statements such as "I want to stay pure" often allow too much latitude. It's too easy to fall into sexually promiscuous behavior or to confuse the other person if you don't spell out what is and is not acceptable. If the person you're dating feels strongly that the boundary line should be drawn more tightly, you should defer to her.

Like physical limits, emotional boundaries should be clear and distinct. There are two major areas of emotional boundaries: conversation (where you express feelings, hopes, desires) and action. For instance, determine which subject matters in conversation would lead you to deeper emotional intimacy than your relationship can handle. Again, *be specific*— and follow through! If you decide at the beginning of your relationship that you will not talk about marriage, don't talk about marriage. When you do become more serious with the right person, there will be plenty of time to discuss such issues.

As far as actions are concerned, agree upon how much time you will spend alone together, with other people, on the phone, and apart. You'll do best if you get to know a person in different contexts. If you balance how often you'll be one-on-one, on group dates, with friends and family, in telephone conversation, and apart from each other, you will be less likely to become emotionally intimate prematurely. Again, we'll be looking more at both physical and emotional boundaries later in the book.

Starting a dating relationship is similar to setting out on a journey with someone else. When you travel by car, you agree upon where you'd like to go and map out how to get there. When you travel by plane or boat, you set the coordinates of your final destination. If the coordinates aren't set correctly, you have a lot more trouble reaching your final destination.

A LITTLE HOW-TO

Prior to moving on, we'd like to highlight some other elements of how to DTR in the beginning. (And you can use these tips for future DTRs, too!)

1. Come to the conversation prepared. You may think it's goofy, but if it will help you, write out what you want to say. You might also want to revisit the guidelines for "What is a DTR" and "When to DTR."

2. Be open to the other person wanting something completely different—in interest, intentions, or boundaries. You just cannot predict another's desires or feelings.

3. Don't get ahead of yourself and try to discuss things that don't apply to your blossoming relationship. Some specifics will need to be hammered out in later DTRs, should your relationship continue to progress.

4. Leave room for the other person to ask questions, and don't be afraid to ask for clarification yourself. You shouldn't leave a DTR wondering, *What does he think about this?* or *Will she feel comfortable with that?*

5. Don't expect a DTR to eliminate all of the messiness of a relationship. You may still wonder what the person thinks when he says x, y, or z. You may be confused by her attitude or reactions. A DTR can establish some essentials, but at the beginning of any relationship you're still dealing with a defined unknown. Only with time will you really come to feel comfortable and at ease with how you are relating.

If your relationship develops, preserve the firm foundation you've built by periodically assessing whether your relationship has grown out of the things you established in your first DTR. Having DTRs as things change and progress will help you keep your finger on the pulse of your relationship and determine if you two are still on the same page.

Where Do We Go from Here?

Years ago, Anne Morrow Lindbergh wrote these insightful words:

> The first part of every relationship is…pure, simple, unencum-
> bered. And then how swiftly the perfect unity is invaded; the rela-
> tionship changes; it becomes complicated, encumbered…. There is
> also a deadweight accumulation, a coating of false values, habits,
> and burdens which blights life. It is this smothering coat that needs
> constantly to be stripped off, in life as well as in relationships.[1]

The "smothering coat" that Lindbergh refers to can be any number of
pressures or mistakes in a relationship. It can be the simple rubs of daily life,
or it can be a major issue like purity. Sometimes, as in the situation of a
couple named Brad and Amber, both the accumulation of time and the
"coating of false values, habits, and burdens" weigh down a relationship.

Brad and Amber began their relationship well. Early on they established boundaries for their relationship in several key areas. They wanted
to stay both physically and emotionally pure, so they talked over what
might lead them down the wrong paths.

Time flew by, and the busyness of life—the demands of day-to-day details—crowded out some of the things Brad and Amber had done in the first stages of their relationship. They assumed, though, that the conversations about boundaries that they'd had long ago would last. Why should they spend time going over their commitments to purity and their emotional guardedness? Nothing had changed.

A few months into their relationship, however, things did start changing. Everything began to feel strained. Brad became easily annoyed at Amber's strong opinions. Amber couldn't stand the fact that Brad suddenly had to be right about everything.

Little disagreements started to turn into knock-down-drag-out fights. Neither wanted to be the first to apologize, so it would often take days for them to reconcile. Sometimes they'd have passionate "makeup make-outs" after their fights, and one thing began to lead to another until they'd crossed the boundaries they'd originally defined.

The weight of their fights and the guilt they carried from going too far physically put a strain on the emotional dynamics of Brad and Amber's relationship. Both started to feel their standards in that area slip as well.

But neither knew what to do. They felt as if they needed to talk, but it seemed easier to put off what they anticipated would be a difficult conversation. They weren't sure if they should just break up; they didn't *want* to. But what could they do to start working through these issues? Where did they go from here?

Brad and Amber had assumed that because they started well, they would continue well. Time and day-to-day living wore down their relationship, but they also didn't exert any effort to keep their original commitments fresh and alive.

Relationships can easily become bogged down; every relationship has the potential to disintegrate. Left alone, a relationship *will* tend to erode. But DTRs can help keep your relationship from slowly crumbling away.

BEATING RELATIONSHIP EROSION

Chuck Swindoll wrote,

> Deterioration is never sudden. No garden "suddenly" overgrows
> with thorns.... No building "suddenly" crumbles. No [relation-
> ship] "suddenly" breaks down.... Slowly, almost imperceptibly
> certain things are accepted that once were rejected. Things once
> considered hurtful are now secretly tolerated. At the outset it ap-
> pears harmless, perhaps even exciting, but the wedge it brings
> leaves a gap that grows wider [until]...the gap becomes a canyon.[2]

What Swindoll describes here is the process of erosion. To erode
means to eat into or eat away, to "destroy by slow disintegration." Over
time, an outside force like water will wear down a surface and destroy it.

I (Jeramy) witnessed the effects of erosion during an eight-month
stint as a landscaper. Hired as part of the grounds maintenance staff at my
home church, I took on the responsibility of keeping the grounds beautiful and healthy. I spent most of those eight months getting ground cover
planted and established. Why? So that the wind and rain that came in
plenty to Northern California would not erode the grounds.

One weekend, however, an outside pipe burst. We're not talking about
an itty-bitty, not-so-important pipe. No, this was a main line. When I
showed up for work on Monday afternoon, a large portion of the hill had
eroded into the middle of the street. It took another staffer and me eight
hours of hard work to shovel the dirt back.

Surfaces disintegrate if they are not protected. Likewise, relationships
can decay and wear away if they are not protected. Wind will come and
rain will fall on every relationship. If a couple isn't careful, circumstances
and time will eat away at the foundation they have built.

Long before scientists studied erosion, the prophet/teacher who penned one of the Bible's books of wisdom warned of this phenomenon. Check out these verses from Proverbs 24:

I passed by the field of the sluggard
And by the vineyard of the man lacking sense,
And behold, it was completely overgrown with thistles;
Its surface was covered with nettles,
And its stone wall was broken down.
When I saw, I reflected upon it;
I looked, and received instruction.
"A little sleep, a little slumber,
A little folding of the hands to rest,"
Then your poverty will come as a robber
And your want like an armed man. (verses 30-34, NASB)

What happened to this garden? Whoever was responsible for maintaining its beauty and life did a little too much afternoon napping. Dale Burke wrote that we can "easily extract a warning from this story, a principle worth remembering. It's that *procrastination leads to devastation.*"[3] Waiting to tend your garden will lead to destruction. Like a garden, a relationship must be consistently tended and maintained. If it is not, it will be destroyed.

And if you'll notice, it doesn't take much to neglect a garden. Only a "*little* sleep, a *little* slumber, a *little* folding of the hands." It's not as if the gardener took off to surf in Maui or ski in Vail for three weeks. It was simply the putting off—the procrastination—that led to breakdown.

Procrastination can be the result of many factors, but most often people put off what is difficult or uncomfortable. Nobody *wants* to get started on that big project that's due in two weeks. It's far more desirable to go out with your friends or read a good book. But when we procrastinate in life or in relationships, things break down and fall apart.

Proverbs 24 helps us visualize what happens in a relationship when we put off what's necessary: Walls break down and weeds grow out of control. Individuals who sidestep consistent maintenance of their relationship are in for tough times. They are even likely to give up. Progress takes work. Growth requires effort. Any couple that assumes they don't need to do anything beyond starting well is in for a serious wake-up call.

So how do you prevent relationship erosion? What can you do to protect your relationship so that procrastination does not wear things down? People try all kinds of things when they notice erosion in nature. Some try to use sandbags and some try to build walls to avoid destruction, but these are temporary solutions. Sandbags and walls will not permanently stop erosion.

There are two good ways to halt the process of erosion. First, if possible, you reroute the forces to keep them away from the vulnerable area. For instance, you channel the flow of water in another direction. This plan requires hard work and ingenuity. Or you can plant grass or ground cover to keep the earth in place. This solution also demands effort and wisdom. You must know the way outside forces affect your surroundings so you can choose the right ground cover. The best thing to do is both redirect the most destructive force *and* protect the surface.

Do these principles work for preventing the erosion of relationships as well? Absolutely! (But you wouldn't want our advice on *literal* gardening. We're total black thumbs!) To avoid the slow disintegration of relationship erosion, start by redirecting things. Redefine the boundaries that you have crossed and reestablish the commitments you first made. Rollo May, a popular psychologist, once commented, "It is an old and ironic habit of human beings to run faster when we have lost our way." In relationships, we have a tendency to press on full-steam ahead when we see erosion occurring. But a person who is lost needs to stop and change directions. A relationship that has lost its way needs to be halted and redirected.

Once you've redirected your relationship, take time to plant some ground cover. By this we mean doing positive, healthy things to build the relationship. Have a plan for your dates and make them purposeful. Set aside constructive times to get acquainted. Build up the other person by supporting his activities and goals. Learn how to encourage the person you're dating. And periodically revisit the initial talk or talks you had about your shared standards and expectations.

Protecting against relationship erosion takes work. People often procrastinate in their relationships because they don't feel like maintaining things. It's too hard or uncomfortable.

The French philosopher Blaise Pascal claimed that it is far easier for people to change their actions than their feelings. Feelings then come with the changed action. So the good news is that as you determine to do things to protect against relationship erosion, you will also begin to feel more able and eager to stay current with the person you're dating. You'll start to choose not to put things off because you've been purposeful in protecting against erosion. Procrastinating won't be as appealing because it may cause you to lose what you've been exerting energy and effort to build up.

We've noticed three factors in particular that lead to procrastination and erosion: conflict, physical boundaries, and excessive emotional attachment. As you look at the next three sections, think about how you can redirect these forces and plant a ground cover that will protect your relationship in the future.

"We're Always Fighting"

Few things are as detrimental to a relationship as constant combat. Whether you're arguing over such trivial issues as where to eat or fighting over major roadblocks such as infidelity and dishonesty, conflict can quickly sour the sweet times of any relationship.

Those of you who have dated the same person for a while may have experienced what some call the honeymoon phase. In the beginning, the person you're with can do no wrong; you're as starry-eyed as two people who have just been married. But the honeymoon phase in dating characteristically comes to an end when a couple has their first bout of fights.

Some daters decide to throw in the towel at the earliest sign of conflict. Their perspective: *Hey, if we're not getting along, we don't have to stay together. We're not married, so we don't have to work through these issues.*

There are definitely times when conflict becomes too weighty for a relationship to continue, and we'll be looking at that in the next chapter. But there are some good reasons to learn how to work through a certain amount of tension and disagreement in your dating relationships. So in this chapter we want to encourage you to use some simple DTR steps to redirect a relationship that is riddled with combat.

First, recognize that some conflict is inevitable. Bad news—we are all sinners. More bad news—our sin means we will argue and disagree in sinful ways in our relationships. A well-known Christian psychologist wrote about still more bad news:

> Show me a relationship that has any time and experience to it and
> I'll show you conflict. It may be overt and loud or quiet as a smol-
> dering fire, but strife is inevitable. We are self-centered people.[4]

So why do we share all this bad news with you? Are we using some weird manipulative psychology to try to scare you away from dating? No, we're just making the point that conflict *will* occur. Recognizing this truth is, in fact, the first step to freedom from conflict. It's also important to remember that conflict doesn't necessarily precipitate "the end." An argument often simply raises a red flag about something that needs to be processed with the person you're dating. As P. B. Wilson advises, "When you see a red flag it doesn't mean you stop everything. It [can] simply mean there are some speed bumps in the road, demanding you move forward at a slower pace."[5] Conflict can present you with a great opportunity to step back, simmer down, and proceed with greater caution. Besides, if things were always smooth in your relationship, you might be tempted to get ahead of yourself.

It's also essential to realize that the anger is not inherently sinful. In Ephesians 4:26 God commands, "Don't sin by letting anger gain control over you" (NLT). Another translation reads, "Be angry, and yet do not sin" (NASB). In other words, anger itself is not sinful. It's how we handle the anger that might allow sin to creep in. God does not want us to be controlled by anger any more than by alcohol, food, or any other *potentially* harmful thing. The Creator of our spirits, minds, and emotions knows that anger arises when life throws us a curve ball. But He wants us to deal with conflict in healthy, godly ways.

In order to do that, you must face conflict head-on. Linus, of the comic strip *Peanuts,* once claimed, "No problem is so big or so complicated that it can't be run away from!" Unfortunately, his philosophy doesn't make for healthy relationships. We need to face conflict directly because without confrontation, pressures mount until a little spark sets off a massive explosion. Unsettled frustrations lead to unrestrained outbursts—raised voices, pointing fingers, hurtful accusations, and name-calling.

So every relationship needs as part of its foundation the commitment to face problems squarely. This is where a DTR comes in handy. A DTR can create an open, positive environment in which to face conflicts, redirect your relationship, and protect it with a ground cover for the future.

We have identified six keys to resolving conflict in healthy, biblical ways. Set a time for a DTR during which you can discuss these techniques. Then you'll be ready to use these tools when conflict arises.

1. Separate the Problem from the Person

We draw this principle from the whole of Scripture: Honor others. If winning an argument comes at the expense of wounding another, you have gained nothing. Conflict does not present a chance for you to prove you're right or to point out someone's faults. You are dealing with a problem to be solved, not a battle to be won. During a DTR to resolve conflict, deal with the *issue* while honoring the worth and significance of the other person.

2. Do All You Can Do

Romans 12:18 calls believers to a high standard: "If it is possible, as far as it depends on you, live at peace with everyone." The phrase *as far as it depends on you* means do as much as you possibly can. Whatever you can control and direct, whatever you can prevent or avoid, you should. Don't merely do what you think is enough to solve the problem. Go beyond that bare minimum and see how your relationship is strengthened.

3. Don't Allow Too Much Time to Elapse

Ephesians 4:26 counsels, "Do not let the sun go down while you are still angry." The longer we wait to deal with a conflict, the harder it gets. The more we stew about differences and frustrations, the less we are able to view them objectively. In a dating relationship, sometimes you can't talk to the person the night the conflict arises. But the principle remains that the sooner you deal with a clash, the better. Don't let frustrations harden into something worse by letting time slip away.

Be aware also that some issues may need to be shelved overnight or over a few nights. All conflicts are not resolvable in one conversation, and forcing a conversation to some kind of "end" can be detrimental to your relationship. Use discernment to decide when to push through a hard talk and when to set aside your issues temporarily to give both people a chance to think and pray.

4. Speak the Truth in Love

This standard comes directly from Scripture (Ephesians 4:15 to be precise). Found in these five words are not one but two keys for healthy conflict resolution. First, be honest about what the problem is. Second, be honest in a loving manner. Again, conflict does not present a battle to be won, but a problem to be solved.

5. Respond in Gentleness to the Anger of Another

What does Scripture have to say about our response to another person's anger? Proverbs 15:1 says, "A gentle answer turns away wrath, but a harsh word stirs up anger." To resolve a conflict, respond gently and calmly to another's irritation. If you choose to respond in anger, you will only stir up more heated emotions.

6. Pick Your Battles

This may seem like a contradiction after we've emphasized facing conflict head-on, but there are times to simply let things go. Some things are just not important enough to discuss. Develop discernment as to which conflicts are worth hashing through and which would be best to let drop. In Proverbs 17:14 we read, "Beginning a quarrel is like opening a floodgate, so drop the matter before a dispute breaks out" (NLT). You don't need to open the floodgate every time. Learn the difference between a conflict that, as it is resolved, will build up your relationship and a petty disagreement that will break it down.

So if you find your relationship stuck because of conflict, take time for a DTR about how you can resolve disagreements. As you commit to these scriptural principles, your relationship can grow in a new and healthier way. A DTR about conflict resolution also covers you for the future because you will have tools at the ready to face the conflicts that will inevitably come.

You Are Not Doomed by Desire

Nothing wields as much erosive force in a relationship as premature physical intimacy. Getting too close physically ushers a huge amount of confusion into a dating relationship, not to mention a tremendous weight of guilt for those who know the Lord and want to obey His commands.

Couples who get too intimate too soon also face questions of trust. After all, if your boyfriend can't control himself physically with you, can you expect him to restrain his desire with others? The same question can be asked about girlfriends!

Intimacy without commitment leads to uncertainty and insecurity and then to jealousy. That's because God created intimacy for a safe and secure relationship. In 1 Corinthians 7, the Lord explains that He intends sexuality, with all its passion and power, to be contained in the only relationship strong enough to keep it—marriage. Outside of that permanent, lifelong commitment, the questions mount: *Will I still be good enough for this person tomorrow? What happens when the fun wears off? Is he looking at that other girl the same way he looked at me when we first started dating?*

We recently watched with deep sadness as two singles we respect and enjoy became caught up in inappropriate sexual expression. It got to the point where they went to Jeramy's office and poured out their guilt, confusion, and frustration.

The young woman in the relationship confessed something that revealed the extent to which impurity can erode and distort a couple: She admitted that she wanted to get pregnant so that she could "keep" the guy, so that he would stay faithful to her. This floored us as well as the young man. How did the relationship progress to the point that she would even think about such a drastic plan?

Most couples won't find themselves in such an extreme situation but may nevertheless find the relationship eroded by excessive physicality. They didn't *intend* for things to progress that way, but their physical relationship seemed to take on a life of its own. We counsel these couples to redefine their boundaries and recommit to the standards of purity God would have for them; we challenge them to recapture a passion for purity, rather than pleasure. Now, we're not going to pull any punches here. This step backward in a physical relationship is DIFFICULT!—with capital letters, exclamation point, and all.

You can compare the progression of a physical relationship to the use of different modes of transportation. When you start life, you crawl everywhere, and then you learn to walk. Walking works for a while until you want to go farther, faster. Then maybe you pick up Rollerblades, a skateboard, or a bike. Finally you begin to drive, and the car replaces your earlier methods of getting from here to there.

Once you have a car or even learn to drive, how easy would it be to go back to crawling everywhere? It's a funny mental picture—a bunch of adults crawling to work. But we think you get the point: It would be extraordinarily difficult to go back.

And once you begin to kiss, it's tough to be satisfied with holding hands. Once you go beyond kissing, a good-night peck is not enough. It is very difficult to become less physical, but it's not impossible. You are not doomed by desire. You have not gone too far to go back. In the Lord's strength, you can restrain yourself and redirect your relationship.

Having a DTR when you're stuck in a rut of being physically

inappropriate can firm up your devotion to the Lord and the other person and solidify your standards to His commands. Here are six guidelines for recapturing your relationship's purity.

1. Confess Your Sin

Go to the Lord on your own first. First John 1:9 proclaims, "If we confess our sins, he is faithful and just and will forgive us our sins and purify us from all unrighteousness." Then come together and acknowledge your mistakes. This is *not* the time, however, to relive things by going into detail about how you've sinned. Simply confess to each other that what you have done grieves God. As you confess, you open the door for change: "Therefore confess your sins to each other and pray for each other so that you may be healed" (James 5:16).

2. Affirm Your Desire to Live Righteously

Great power comes with verbalizing your pledges to the Lord. The psalms are full of people voicing their longing to keep vows they've made to God. Making your standards known to another person, especially your date, encourages you to keep those standards more steadfastly. May the words from Psalm 61:8 be your hope as well as your promise: "I [will] ever sing praise to your name *and fulfill my vows day after day*" (emphasis added).

3. Pray for Each Other

James 5:16 also inspires this essential. When you have confessed your sin and affirmed your desire to move forward in holiness, commit yourselves to pray for each other. Because of the special intimacy created by prayer, though, we suggest that you spend only a short time praying together. Instead, devote yourselves to praying separately and every day for each other's purity.

4. Stop Any Physical Contact That Leads to Impurity

When Jesus encountered a sexually promiscuous woman in John 8, He did not condemn her. But He did tell her, "Go now and leave your life of sin" (verse 11). When you have confessed to the Lord and received His forgiveness, He tells you as well, "Leave your life of sin." Make the commitment as a couple to stop doing the things that have taken you close to crossing—or even across—your boundaries.

5. Discuss Ways to Change Your Behavior

In other words, repent of what you've done. To repent literally means to turn away from sinful behavior altogether. It means doing a 180-degree turn. Repentance doesn't mean merely saying you're sorry; it means changing what you do. In Acts 26:20, the apostle Paul "preached that [all] should repent and turn to God and prove their repentance by their deeds." As a couple, talk about what situations have led you to impurity in the past. Agree together to go down a different road in the future. Then go forward and prove your repentance by your deeds.

6. Determine That You Will Both Ask for Help

It's difficult, if not impossible, to stay pure without the assistance of others. You need the prayer support of other Christians. The second half of James 5:16 proclaims, "The prayer of a righteous man is powerful and effective." It also helps to be accountable to someone who will ask you how things are going. As you submit your relationship to God as well as to outside counsel and evaluation, it can be greatly strengthened and reordered.

These guidelines are essential to remember as you DTR about your physical relationship. If a DTR *doesn't* seem effective in helping you stay pure, however, you may want to assess your relationship with the questions and answers presented in the next chapter. Remember, keeping your physical relationship pure is one of the best ways to prevent relationship erosion.

EMOTIONAL BAGGAGE

Once when traveling through Europe, we walked for several miles from the train station to our hotel. Truth be told, it was the place we *thought* our hotel was. Our backs and shoulders were aching from the weight of our bags, but we kept pressing on, assuming that we'd be able to lay our burdens down once we arrived. Not until we had trudged clear through the city did we finally stop to reassess. We looked at the map again and determined that where the hotel should have been, no hotel stood. We had to lug ourselves and our bags back to the center of the city and find another place to stay.

Navigating a city with baggage loaded on you isn't easy. Negotiating a relationship with the weight of emotional baggage is also arduous—and emotional baggage is much more difficult to see than a duffel bag! Yet poorly defined emotional boundaries can weigh a relationship down until it breaks.

We see two primary causes of emotional heaviness. The first is unmet and undefined expectations. We all have certain ideas about how a relationship should go. When things go according to our plan, our emotional response is upbeat. The problem is that most relationships *don't* proceed as both parties would like. Usually one if not both partners are disappointed when they compare what they imagined would happen with what is actually happening.

Unmet and undefined expectations can show up in your reaction to something as simple as a gift—or the lack of a gift. Perhaps Valentine's Day comes and you get nada. You start to wonder why you're so bothered by the "thoughtlessness" of your boyfriend or girlfriend. Maybe your sig-

nificant other consistently forgets important dates or fails to call when he
said he would. Perhaps the relationship is not progressing as fast as you
want it to, and while the other person seems to be satisfied with where you
are, you just can't shake the feeling that you're not getting what you want.

The second major cause of emotional baggage in a relationship is uneven commitment. That is, one person views the relationship far more
seriously than the other. Uneven commitment eventually leads to feelings
of resentment on one side and feelings of desperation on the other. The
person who views the relationship as casual begins to begrudge the weightiness with which the other perceives things. The person who wants more
from the relationship pushes to make it more serious.

It's been said that people crave what they can't attain, but disrespect
what they can't escape. If a person feels she cannot escape the extreme anxiety that weighs down a relationship, she will begin to lose interest, increasing the desperation of her partner.

Unmet expectations and unequal commitment often go together.
Josh McDowell wrote about this correlation:

> You have a relationship in which one party is much more serious
> and interested than the other. Several basic causes exist for this kind
> of a situation. For example, a person may enter a relationship sim-
> ply because it's convenient. For some, a dating relationship can be a
> means of dealing with loneliness. For others it can be a ticket to din-
> ners and entertainment. Now that does not necessarily mean that the
> other party is being "used." It depends on one's expectations.[6]

Couples who get stuck in relationships because their emotions have
become heavy baggage need to redirect the way they relate on an emotional level. We've come up with five directives that can help you redefine
a relationship in which emotions have gone overboard. The first two you

cover as individuals during a time of personal reflection. The last three are subjects for you to discuss with the person you're dating.

1. Determine Whether Your Feelings Match the Level of the Relationship

Are you obsessing about marriage when your relationship is still in the casual dating stage? Are you in an exclusive relationship with someone you don't feel strongly about? Do you feel out of step with where your relationship is? If you're having a hard time with this assessment, talk to a trusted, more mature Christian. Bounce your feelings and frustrations off that person, and ask him to help you see where your feelings may be out of step.

2. Ask Yourself, "Am I Being Selfish?"

Self-focus creates emotional baggage in many relationships. Before you talk with the person you're dating, determine if you want more from the relationship than is healthy. Are you consumed with having your needs met? First Corinthians 13 reminds us that love "does not seek its own" (verse 5, NASB). Pray for discernment to recognize where you may have acted in selfishness. Renew a commitment to look to the needs of others, not just your own (see Philippians 2:4).

3. Lay the Baggage Down

Acknowledge what's weighing on you. Express where you are and allow the other person time to process what you're saying. Ask about your date's level of commitment and degree of expectation. Make sure she's heard and understood you, and let her ask you the same questions. Hebrews 12:1 encourages believers to travel light: "Let us throw off everything that hinders and the sin that so easily entangles." Poorly defined emotional standards can hinder and entangle your relationship. Throw off that excess weight!

4. Agree to Take a Step Back

You'll be amazed by how drastically your perspective changes when you remove yourself from the intensity of the situation. During your DTR, you might decide to spend a bit of time apart or to cut back on the one-on-one time you've had together. You can also assess whether the amount of time you spend on the phone is helping or hindering your relationship. Agreeing to take action together will help relieve some of the tension and pressure that has built up.

5. Talk About Your Talk

Lest you think you've been warped into *The Idiot's Guide to DTR*, let us explain that little statement. What you two talk about together affects the emotional heaviness of your relationship. In fact, this point is important enough that we're going to explore it further in chapter 8. For now, keep in mind that a DTR can help you recognize where you've allowed yourself latitude in your conversation. Together you can agree to stop talking loosely about those topics that are not helpful or healthy. Pray with David: "May the words of my mouth and the meditation of my heart be pleasing in your sight, O LORD" (Psalm 19:14).

◆

A DTR can help you get back on the same emotional page with the person you're dating. That's why it's wise, every so often, to assess your relationship's emotional weight. Don't wait to refocus your emotional intensity when necessary.

You may find that you as a couple struggle more with one factor behind relationship erosion than with others. Or you might discover that your relationship seems to cycle in and out of these different areas as it progresses. The key is to be alert to the forces that might break down what you have and to take actions that will help you now and in the future.

The End?

As confusing and complex as relationships can be, it's sometimes startling to remember that every relationship has one of only two outcomes: You break up or you get married. At some point, your dating relationship *will* end. It may end in friendship or distance, or it may end in marriage.

Chances are, if you've dated more than one person, you've come to a crossroads at some point where you're forced to determine which direction a relationship should go: Are we serious enough to get married, or should we move on? If you've ever found yourself in such a situation, you might have felt frustrated because you didn't have a lot of guidance for determining whether you should try to redefine things, take a more serious step, or simply call it quits.

Our aim is for this chapter to provide you with counsel and some effective methods of evaluation to help you determine whether a dating relationship should end completely, should continue as it is, or should end in marriage.

CALLING IT QUITS

First we'll look at reasons why a couple might completely end a relationship. Sometimes forces can erode a relationship so much that you start to wonder if the relationship can survive—or should survive. You may wrestle with questions about whether you should stay together. It can be extremely difficult to make that final decision, particularly if you have been dating the person for a long time.

We'd like to present you with six common reasons why couples question whether they should continue dating. Of course, the reasons for considering a breakup are as varied as the couples themselves. But you may find yourself now or in the future identifying with some of these experiences as you evaluate a relationship that might be poised to end.

Two Roads Diverging

We've known Tanya and Trevor for years. We watched their friendship blossom into romance, we watched them get together, and we gave them counsel throughout their year-plus relationship.

When Trevor's circumstances changed and he moved out of state, many of their friends hoped they would make it. Neither Trevor nor Tanya had serious reservations about carrying on a long-distance relationship. They both felt it *could* work, and they were willing to try for as long as it seemed healthy.

For a few months they continued to enjoy each other through phone and e-mail, and occasionally they had the chance to see each other in person. But as time progressed and they thought about their stage of life, Tanya and Trevor came to the conclusion that they were headed in different directions. They were not only apart physically, but they felt the paths they'd chosen—Trevor with semipro or pro sports and Tanya wanting a career of her own—were going to conflict. Continuing to invest in their relationship would only lead them closer to marriage, which neither saw as an option in the near future.

As they prayed about what they should do, they felt a peace about breaking up and staying friends. They both thought something might happen later in life, but they didn't want to expect or count on that.

We could not have respected Tanya and Trevor's decision more. Each sought God's will, surrendered someone dear to His care, and received His peace and clarity.

In Amos 3:3, the prophet asks, "Can two people walk together without agreeing on the direction?" (NLT). A relationship is about walking together through life. If you're headed in different directions, you will not be able to walk together.

Sometimes people can't walk together because of physical distance. When you're in different locations, it's difficult to maintain a close relationship. Long-distance relationships take their toll.

That's not to say that it's impossible for a couple to succeed when they're separated by miles. We observed a wonderful, godly couple date during high school, go away to different colleges for four years, and then marry after graduating. But key in their relationship was a shared commitment to life direction. They both wanted to serve God in some variety of full-time ministry. They wanted to raise a family who would serve and honor the Lord. They were walking in step with each other even though they were separated physically.

For many, however, a long-distance relationship will not work, and there is nothing wrong with that. The strain of long drives and extended phone calls affects some people more deeply than others. You need to be honest about your own capacity to relate across the miles. If you, like Tanya and Trevor, determine that a long-distance relationship is not God's will for you, it's time to end things.

Far more important than assessing whether you're headed in two different physical directions, however, is discerning whether your heart passions are leading you to part ways. French thinker Antoine de Saint-Exupéry once wrote, "To love does not mean simply to look at one another but to look together in the same direction."[1] Love must involve not only a shared direction but also a shared vision for that direction. When you and the person you're relating to see the world entirely differently, you're in for some difficulties.

Imagine a couple trying to build a life when the man is a committed military officer and the woman wants to stay in her hometown. She's not interested in moving from place to place and starting a new life wherever her husband is stationed. What about a woman whose heart's desire is to serve on the mission field, but the man she's dating wants to practice criminal law? What happens if you find out that the person you're dating doesn't want a family at all, yet you've always dreamed of having four or more kids?

If you find that your vision for the world and the future differs too drastically from that of the person you're dating, you have two options: You can alter your own vision (you cannot expect to change another person's vision), or you can end the relationship and seek a person who is walking and looking in the same direction you are.

The ultimate question you need to ask is whether God would have you surrender your vision or surrender the person you're with. Answering that question will lead you to a decision about whether to end the relationship.

There's one more important point: If you discover that the person you're dating is no longer headed in the same spiritual direction you are, it's most likely time to break up. When someone ceases to pursue the things of the Lord, you cannot continue in close relationship with that person without being impacted yourself.

You can observe someone's spiritual direction by watching him in five different areas—interaction with the Word of God, worship, prayer, fellowship with others, and sharing the faith. If the person you're dating no longer exhibits a passion to turn his eyes from worthless things and refresh his commitments to the Lord, and if he no longer brings the Word, hidden in his memory, to mind at crucial moments or uses Scripture to quickly challenge and redirect any decisions that could take him down the wrong path,[2] beware of the spiritual direction in which he is heading.

Also pay attention if the person you're dating is not grieved by sin or her behavior begins to reflect a carnal mind-set. As Paul noted, "The sinful nature desires what is contrary to the Spirit, and the Spirit what is contrary to the sinful nature" (Galatians 5:17). A person walking in the Spirit will not continually desire what the sinful nature lusts to have.

A person alive in Christ will desire His Word, long to worship Him, eagerly pray, always submit to corporate and private fellowship, and demonstrate a desire to share the faith. It's not that a person will ever do these things *perfectly*. It's the bent of the heart that matters.

If you and the person you're dating are headed in different directions geographically, looking in different life directions, or walking opposite ways spiritually, it's often best to end the relationship before it progresses further.

Habits Are Hard to Break

The first time Becca laid eyes on Justin, she felt her stomach drop with excitement. Justin appealed to Becca's every sense. He had a dark, somewhat mysterious look about him, and a strong athletic build. She loved hearing his deep, masculine voice from down the hallway at work.

Becca and Justin didn't even work in the same department. But when it came time for the company holiday party, a coworker finagled things so that Becca and Justin drove together. The two ended up at each other's side the whole evening and had a great time. Justin asked Becca if he could take her out the next weekend, and a relationship was born.

At first Becca felt a sense of accomplishment at having snagged this guy she'd so admired. But she quickly discovered that physical attraction doesn't go very far in building a real relationship. It didn't take long for her to realize that Justin not only didn't share her faith but had little interest in God at all. For that matter, Justin didn't seem interested in much of anything. He never had a whole lot to say, and Becca constantly felt the pressure of having to carry the conversation.

But Justin and Becca got into a routine, and their relationship, as poor as it was, became familiar and easy. They were established as a couple, and Becca was in the habit of spending time with Justin, calling him, and kissing him.

Would you believe that Becca didn't end the relationship for over six months? Though he bored her in conversation and did not share her faith—which she claimed was the most important thing in her life— Justin had become a habit for Becca.

When she finally decided it was time to end things, Becca found it more difficult than she'd imagined. It felt comfortable and safe to have Justin by her side. It was hard for her to imagine being without a boyfriend.

It's time to end things when you know that being in a relationship has simply become a habit, when doing the familiar thing is easier than doing the difficult thing of breaking up and being on your own again. An old saying teaches, "The wise does at once what the fool does last." Eventually, a relationship that's built only on familiarity and habit will lead to a bitter end—either in a drawn-out breakup or, worse, an unhappy marriage. Far better to exercise wisdom and end things now than to hold on to a relationship simply because it feels safe.

The danger of not ending the relationship sooner rather than later is that once something's become a habit, it becomes more and more difficult to separate yourself. The American educator Horace Mann once said that habit is a cable: We weave a thread of it every day, and at last we cannot break it.

So if you find yourself holding on to a relationship that's convenient, familiar, and secure, but not ultimately fulfilling or godly, get out now. Exercise wisdom: Do today what will save you from greater heartbreak later.

Constant Combat

In the previous chapter, we talked about how a Christian couple can benefit from learning to work through conflict. But what happens when the tension simply overwhelms your interaction? Is it godlier to remain in the relationship and persevere through every battle? Not necessarily. There are times when constant combat signals that the relationship should end.

This was the case for Tim and Cathy. Both of them were argumentative types, and their relationship seemed fraught with conflict from the get-go. But they enjoyed each other's sense of humor and found each other physically and spiritually attractive.

The emotional attraction, though, couldn't go anywhere because they bickered over every little thing. The minutiae of day-to-day living— questions like what movie to see that night or which CD to listen to in the car—became springboards for violent discussion on what was "best" or "right." And it didn't stop on that level. The two always found themselves on opposite sides of issues. Theological questions that mattered deeply to both of them became major battlefields.

You may be wondering why this couple got together in the first place or how they survived even one date. But Tim and Cathy thought that things could get better if they'd just… Just what? Just change so that they felt the same as the other person? Or just give in every time the other picked a fight? What were they "just" supposed to do?

Before long, Tim and Cathy decided to break up. Besides not having any fun in their relationship, they were also not able to honor each other in the Lord when they were together as a couple.

These two made the right decision. The mix of their two personalities simply did not lead to harmony and joy. Both later met people with whom they could find greater peace.

If you've tried to resolve conflict in the biblical ways we mentioned in chapter 5 but have found that you continue to face battle after battle, stop and evaluate your relationship using the following questions:

- Do you constantly have to clarify yourself or say "I'm sorry" for yesterday's argument?
- Do you find yourself or the other person bent on picking everything apart or hashing and rehashing dead issues?
- How important is it to you to be right in a given situation? How important is it to the person you're dating to be right?
- How many phone calls do you spend in silence or misunderstanding?
- How many times have you threatened to break up or suggested, "Maybe we should think about spending some time apart"?

Reflect on your answers to these questions to determine whether your level of conflict has gotten out of hand. A certain level of conflict can be healthy for anyone; it can sharpen and shape you. But taken to the next level of intensity, conflict tears you down and tears you apart. Staying in a combative relationship and trying to make your personalities gel is not "spiritual." In fact, doing so can be destructive to your spirit as well as to the other person.

Think of Proverbs 17:14: "Starting a quarrel is like breaching a dam." When you establish a pattern of quarreling, the argumentation can take on a momentum and energy of its own, like waters rushing from a broken dam. If you feel overwhelmed by the torrential flood of combat in your relationship, you should consider bringing the relationship to an end.

Proverbs 17 also teaches, "He who loves a quarrel loves sin" (verse 19). If you find yourself enjoying tension and picking fights or if you notice that the person you are dating seems bent on looking for the next argument, you should contemplate ending the relationship.

Remember these final lessons from Proverbs. In 19:13 the writer observes, "A quarrelsome wife is like a constant dripping." And God considers this point important enough to repeat it a couple of chapters later in 21:9: "Better to live on a corner of the roof than share a house with a quarrelsome wife." And lest you think you're off the hook, guys, we're quite certain the same could be said of living with a quarrelsome husband.

If dating relationships are supposed to lead to marriage, you should not remain where you find "constant dripping." Such relationships will lead you only to the kind of marriage in which you'd be better off living on the roof than under it with the person you chose.

When Hot Is Too Heavy

Nothing grieves us quite like seeing those we love spiral out of control into sexual immorality. Not only do these friends' relationships end in heartbreak and guilty frustration, but their spirits are wounded by continually living as they know they should not.

We know you're not supposed to have favorites when you work with people, but Erica and Lance were two of our favorite people to minister to. Over the years we'd spent quite a bit of time with them and their families. Intelligent and interesting conversationalists, they were solid Christians who wanted to dialogue about the things of faith and what could strengthen their relationship with Jesus. These funny, lighthearted, and dynamic people could brighten an evening with humor and laughter.

When Erica and Lance decided to start dating, even their families were buzzing with the *m* word. Their personalities seemed well suited for each other, and they even wanted to pursue the same career path in full-time ministry.

Erica and Lance dated for several months before anyone guessed there might be a problem in their relationship. At one point Erica had taken Jerusha aside at church and asked about physical issues, but that conversation hadn't given Jerusha a clear indication that the two were struggling intensely.

But they were. Every time they got together, they battled the desires of their flesh and often found themselves failing. They tried a number of avenues to recapture the purity of their relationship, but none alleviated the pressure of their physical relationship.

They eventually sought counsel from Jeramy and expressed the heavy guilt they felt. Both had been involved in leadership positions at the church. They felt as if they were living a lie—leading on Sundays and engaging in sexual sin most other days of the week.

Erica and Lance could point out ways their excessive physicality was damaging their relationship. They could quote the Scriptures on sexual purity. They *knew* what to do, but it came down to whether they would obey.

Erica and Lance continued to date for a bit longer, but they ultimately ended the relationship because the sin did not stop. Although they both experienced heartbreaking emotions, their decision was mature, right, and pleasing to God.

The Lord warns against sexual promiscuity fifty times in the New Testament alone. Promiscuity can be defined as reckless sexual behavior. If you are part of a relationship that includes careless sexual behavior, you must consider breaking up.

In His Word God commands us to "flee from sexual immorality. All other sins a man commits are outside his body, but he who sins sexually sins against his own body" (1 Corinthians 6:18). Ephesians 5 goes even further: "But among you there must not even be a hint of sexual immorality…because [this is] improper for God's holy people" (verse 3).

If you've pursued the means of healing and restoration we suggested in the last chapter but find yourself blowing it again and again, stop kidding yourself! As believers, we need to make God's will our top priority: We *must* obey Him. Samuel Dickey Gordon wrote, "Anything that does not align with obedience to Him is a waste of time and energy."[3]

If you find that your relationship is keeping you from obeying the Lord, it's time to end things…*now.* "Instant obedience is the only kind of obedience there is, for *delayed* obedience is disobedience."[4]

God promises that obedience will bring His special and precious blessing. The prophet Isaiah phrased it beautifully: "If you are willing and obedient, you will eat the best from the land" (1:19). You will not go without or be deprived. You will have the best!

Yes, it will be tough to end the relationship. But "every difficult task that comes across your path—every one that you would rather not do, that will take the most effort, cause the most pain, and be the greatest struggle—brings a blessing with it. And refusing to do it regardless of the personal cost is to miss the blessing."[5]

Don't miss God's blessing by clinging to a relationship given over to sexual immorality. Your grief in letting go will not be wasted. In 2 Corinthians 7:10, the Lord promises, "Godly sorrow brings repentance that leads to salvation and leaves no regret."

Unfaithful

When I (Jerusha) was in high school, I dated someone who was quite a bit older than me. (Don't get me wrong! He wasn't forty or anything. He was just a senior when I was a freshman.) We met during rehearsals for a musical and clicked on a number of different levels. We both enjoyed dancing, singing, and loved the Los Angeles Lakers.

Though Sean hadn't been involved in church for a long time, he started coming faithfully with me. Also, I set some pretty strict boundaries for our physical relationship, concerned that Sean, being older, might want or expect more than I knew the Lord would have me give. To my amazement, I never felt an ounce of pressure from Sean. Physical issues just didn't come up. We spent our time laughing, playing, and enjoying each other's company.

The only uncomfortable dynamic of our relationship came from what I assumed to be an outside source. A former girlfriend of Sean's, whom friends told me "couldn't let go," would stare at me with an evil eye and spread nasty rumors. Allison tried to make me feel as awkward as possible whenever she could. Most of the time she succeeded. But the situation didn't really cause me to consider breaking up with Sean.

That is, until I got a phone call from Evil Eye herself. Trust me, I nearly dropped the phone when I heard her voice on the other end. I couldn't believe this girl would harass me at home, too. But Allison didn't call to stalk me. She just wanted to inform me that she and Sean had been "hooking up on the side." With some bitterness, Allison confided, "I guess everything he can't get from you he's willing to take from me." I didn't have to ask her to explain. I felt sick to my stomach. So Sean had been physical with Allison because he hadn't been "getting any" from me. All I could think was *Yuck!*

We've been floored and deeply saddened by e-mails we've received from people asking if they should break up with a boyfriend or girlfriend who's been unfaithful. A surprising number of people out there have this question. As we read these stories, we try to evaluate each situation individually. To follow are the ways we attempt to help people discern if it is, indeed, time to end the relationship.

First, acknowledge that there has been a serious breach of trust. Trust forms the foundation of a healthy relationship, and unfaithfulness wounds that basic part of a person's heart that longs to be respected, cared for, and protected.

Acknowledging and assessing your pain may help you see instantly that your dating relationship is not worth continuing. Or you may still have some questions, particularly if you've invested a great deal in the relationship. *Can't a person change? Just because she did this now doesn't mean that she'll do this for life—or does it?*

If you find yourself asking these questions, we suggest a twofold evaluation. First, determine whether the act of unfaithfulness is a fault or a flaw. A person who makes a mistake is different from a person who lives a pattern of sin. If the person who's been unfaithful exhibits genuine repentance, the relationship may be salvageable. If this act of unfaithfulness has been a repeat performance, though, it may indicate a pattern. No one should stay in a dating relationship with someone who makes a habit of infidelity.

The second part of the evaluation focuses on you. Ask yourself, *Am I willing to take a risk on this person?* If you intend to see how far the relationship can go, even to marriage, you must be willing to accept that the actions of the person you are dating now could determine his future deeds.

There is no doubt that unfaithfulness in dating increases the uncertainty of a potential future commitment. A person who shows herself faithful during dating can be trusted much more readily than one who does not.

Those who can endure the risk with peace and confidence may determine that they can persevere in the relationship. But if you find yourself consumed with anxiety about this person's future devotion, you've chosen the path of fear, worry, and unease. It's time to end the relationship if you cannot be sure about the pattern of a person's life or your ability or willingness to endure possible further pain.

If you do not end the relationship, jealousy can enter the picture and eat at your ability to live freely and joyfully. You may also begin to struggle with insecurities, which will further cloud your vision and disintegrate your trust. Often people who have been betrayed ask, *Was it something I did? Am I destined to be cheated on by others? Am I not worthy of better treatment?* If you are going down the road of jealousy or insecurity, end things and guard your heart.

Whatever you choose in your individual circumstances, take some time for healing and the restoration of your own soul. You *are* worth too much to subject yourself to such treatment from an unfaithful partner. God will use this pain to teach you, and as you grieve and heal, we pray that He may reveal His faithfulness to you more than He ever has.

Fear Factor

We'd like to give you one final glimpse into a relationship that needed to end, this one because of fear. Fear has no place in relationships built on the faultless love of Christ. First John 4:18 tells us that "perfect love expels all fear" (NLT). But fear can become an overwhelming factor in partnerships not centered on that flawless standard.

Peter and Susan's relationship highlights the detrimental effects of fear on two levels. Let us share their story with you.

Peter and Susan dated in an admittedly reckless fashion. They didn't define their boundaries very clearly, and only a few months into their relationship, they were way too intimate—physically as well as emotionally. After a year of dating, things had progressed to the point that neither had any other meaningful friendships. They spent all of their time together, and their emotional attachment seemed unbreakable. Their physical relationship only made things worse.

Despite these obvious indicators that their relationship was headed down a destructive path, the first time Susan realized that things might be unhealthy was when she heard Peter's mother start a sentence with "Well, when you guys get married…"

Susan couldn't get her mind off those words. She suddenly felt trapped. She had not thought about the future much until this point, and when Peter's mom simply assumed that they would be together, it scared her.

Susan started to reevaluate their relationship, and she began to see some of the red flags that pastors, friends, and family members had been pointing out to her along the way. She realized that she didn't want to spend the rest of her life with Peter, but she was afraid to cut things off. She shared with Jerusha that she didn't know what life would be like without Peter. She also experienced deep fears about her ability to make or renew friendships. She'd invested so much in her relationship with Peter that she was afraid she'd forgotten how to be a friend, especially a friend to other women. She felt paralyzed.

Then something happened that shocked Susan into a different level of fear altogether. One evening she and Peter got into a fight because of some of the tensions that had been brewing beneath the surface. In the course of the argument, Peter struck Susan. He immediately apologized and told her that he didn't mean to harm her. He admitted he was out of control.

But none of the words Peter spoke could calm Susan's heart. She couldn't believe that he'd hit her. She never imagined that she could be so terrified of a person—or of what might happen now if she did end their relationship.

It took Susan a few days to face Peter again. She did end the relationship with him, and as she expected, he did not take it well. After they broke up he called numerous times a day, and at one point he even parked his car outside her house for almost an entire night.

The fear Susan experienced crippled her for a long time. It took months of healing before she could let go and trust that God would protect her.

God does not intend for relationships to bring fear. A healthy relationship will be free of fear, whether that fear is prompted by a physical, emotional, or psychological threat. Fear indicates that something has gone askew in the relationship.

If you ever find yourself in a relationship where you fear for your future—because you've abandoned your other relationships, because you don't know how you could live without this person, or whatever may be the case—it's probably time to end that relationship.

And should any boyfriend or girlfriend you date abuse you in any way, not only should you report the incident to someone in authority—a pastor, an older family member, a police officer—but you also need to cut ties with the abusive person. Even if someone genuinely experiences sorrow and expresses the desire to repent, you need to separate yourself so that both of you might heal.

God "did not give us a spirit of timidity [fear], but a spirit of power, of love and of self-discipline" (2 Timothy 1:7). It will take power, love, and self-discipline to end a fear-based relationship. You will also need power, love, and self-discipline to move on after such an experience. Praise God that He provides! We do not have to live in fear. We do not have to relate to others in fear.

The greatest truth you can cling to is that you are not alone. You will not be alone when you break up with your girlfriend or boyfriend. God will never forsake you in your time of need. Grab hold of this promise from the book of Isaiah: "So do not fear, for I am with you; do not be dismayed, for I am your God. I will strengthen you and help you; I will uphold you with my righteous right hand" (Isaiah 41:10).

God will hold you up with His strength, and He will give you the courage you need to end a relationship that is not grounded in His faultless love, a love which drives away fear. You are *not* alone—even when a relationship ends.

An End That's Really a Beginning

We recognize that some people reading this book may be heading in the opposite direction of this chapter's topic. You may be considering marriage, not breaking up.

We'd like to include the story of a couple of our friends, Rick and Cathy, who recently pondered whether the time was right to "end" their dating relationship and get engaged. Here's what Rick told us a couple of months ago:

> I just have to tell you I'm in love. I never thought it would happen
> so soon, but Cathy is just the most amazing woman of God. She's
> graduating in the spring and already has a job with a Christian
> organization that runs English camps for kids in developing
> nations. Cathy and I met last year on campus, and we have been
> dating for about nine months. I know that seems like a small
> amount of time, but I really love this woman. I think I want to
> marry her. I still have a year left of school. (I messed around a
> bunch my freshman year and now have to take a fifth year at the
> university.) I have a good part-time job at a church leading wor-
> ship, and I plan to become a music minister when I have my
> degree and when God allows. But I'm a little nervous about getting
> married. I'm only twenty-two. My twenty-six-year-old brother isn't
> even married yet. Still, I love Cathy so much. I sound like a fool, I
> know. I just don't know if I'm mature enough to get married. I
> don't know what I need to be married. How can you tell if you're
> "ready"? People keep telling me that I should wait until I get my
> degree, but that's a whole year from now. It's not that I'm unwilling
> to wait, but I would love to marry Cathy tomorrow, if I could.
> How do I know when I can propose? Do you think I'm ready?

We took some time to process what we knew of Rick and Cathy, and then we wrote this response:

Rick, one thing is for sure: You're not ashamed to admit you're crazy for Cathy. This may surprise you, but fear of actually committing to the feelings of love is one thing that keeps young men from getting engaged and married.

We wish that we could tell you for certain whether you are mature enough and whether your professed love is true enough to marry Cathy tomorrow as you desire. Unfortunately, we can barely offer even a speculation on those matters, which are definitely between you and the Lord. But we *can* give you some things to consider as well as some ways to wade through the issues you'll need to settle before you "drop the rock."

First, we want to tell you that the best way to determine whether you are ready for marriage is to spend time in prayer— *lots* of time in prayer! Listen to the Lord. Read His Word. Seek His face and His will. His guidance is what you need.

Second, we encourage you to get involved in a mentoring relationship with an older man in the Lord (if you're not already). Someone—preferably a married man—who's walked with Christ longer than you have. Someone, also, who *knows* you. It could be a family member, a youth pastor, a professor, really any mature man of faith.

For Jeramy, it was absolutely essential that he have an older man guiding him through our dating and up to our engagement. Ultimately, it was this mentor who asked Jeramy, "What are you waiting for?"

Jeramy couldn't think of anything that was holding him back

from proposing. We'd encourage you to ponder this very same question: What's holding you back?

In order to help you think through some things that *might* be holding you back, here are a few questions worth considering:

- ▼ Are you confident that you want to spend the rest of your life with this woman?
- ▼ How well do you know Cathy?
  - What kind of time have you spent together? We only dated for six months before our engagement, yet we spent true quality time together, getting to know each other over long walks and talks. If we had spent those six months in movie theaters, we probably would not have been able to get to know each other so well.
  - Do you know others who know Cathy? Her family? Friends?
  - What do these people say about her?
- ▼ How would you characterize the health of your relationship emotionally, spiritually, and physically?
- ▼ What do your families think about your relationship? What do your friends say?
- ▼ Are you willing to ask Cathy's father for his daughter's hand? Are you confident he would say yes?
- ▼ How would your job at the church or your schooling be affected if you were to marry Cathy?
  - Would the church support your engagement and allow you to keep your current job?
  - Would you lose any financial aid from the college if you were to marry?
  - Would you be able to finish school?

- Would you be willing to sacrifice your own agenda if your spouse needed you? For example, would you be willing to quit school because of some crisis in your wife's life or your family's life?

▼ Can you support Cathy financially? We know that she has a job, but if she were to be laid off or disabled, it would be your responsibility as the head of your family to provide for her.

▼ Could you support a family financially? You never know what might happen… Jerusha's parents had their first child nine months and two weeks after their honeymoon!

▼ Do you have money to pay for a wedding ring and ceremony? Not all bride's parents are able to finance a wedding.

▼ Finally—and most important—how does Cathy feel about all of this?

We cannot encourage you enough to prayerfully consider each of these questions and, when you're "done," to pray some more.

A couple of months later Rick flew out to New York to meet with Cathy's parents and ask for their blessing before he proposed to Cathy. They were completely supportive and enjoyed helping their future son-in-law get the last-minute details together.

Later that week Rick took Cathy on an all-day adventure, which ended in his proposal that she be his wife for better or for worse. She said yes!

We were delighted when we heard the news from Rick. The man who had been mentoring him was able to do Rick and Cathy's premarital counseling, and Rick and Cathy went ahead and set a wedding date.

Rick's concerns about timing and maturity were good ones for him to work through. He and Cathy chose to take the risk and get engaged. Now newlyweds sharing a life in ministry, Rick and Cathy were just a short time ago, like many couples, questioning whether engagement was the logical next step.

We encouraged Rick to make a decision after much prayer and consideration because sometimes not deciding or delayed deciding can damage a relationship. A couple can get to the point where the health and vitality of their relationship stagnates because neither is willing to make the life decision to commit.

If you have been dating for a while and your circumstances seem to point toward your being ready for marriage, yet you continue to wonder whether you should get engaged, first trust that God will give you the wisdom and discernment you need when you need it. He gave it to us, He gave it to Rick and Cathy, and He will be faithful to guide you, too.

Don't allow your relationship to come to a halt or fall into limbo simply because you "don't know." As we suggested to Rick, do all you can to discover what route God would have you take. Often, the longer a couple dates, the tougher it becomes to decide whether to get engaged or to break up.

When you make the decision to get engaged, your dating relationship "ends," but a whole new—and very exciting—relationship begins. That relationship can and should be defined by continued research, lots of prayer, and (we *highly* recommend) premarital counseling. Our best to those of you who decide you're not waiting for anything!

Surviving a Breakup

You're probably familiar with the Alfred Lord Tennyson quote "'Tis better to have loved and lost than never to have loved at all." When it comes to dating, some might question whether this poetic expression rings true. The drama and pain of a breakup can be enough to make some question whether it is better to avoid dating relationships altogether.

The reality is, if you are going to date, you are most likely going to have to break up. Unless you marry the first person you date, knowing how to end a relationship well is an invaluable tool.

Some people assume that a courtship-only approach to romantic relationships will shield them from breakups. Even with the involvement of parents, pastors, and others, a courting couple may still find they need to end their relationship.

It would be wonderful if every relationship—whether leading to marriage or concluding with a couple going their separate ways—ended happily ever after. After all, isn't that the ideal? Love isn't supposed to be painful, is it?

Ultimately, no. That's not how God, who *is* Love, designed the world. But we don't think it's a big surprise to you that sin messed up the perfection God intended for His children: "For all have sinned and fall short of the glory of God" (Romans 3:23). *All* have sinned. Every single one of us is flawed and broken. Even Paul confessed in Philippians that he had yet to attain what he desired—perfect obedience, perfect submission, perfect fellowship.

So we're still under construction. This means that pain will be mixed with joy in our relationships. Both people will make mistakes. Things won't always go the way we hoped. You can't expect to do everything right, to discern every issue correctly, or to relate to others perfectly. What matters is how you react to the ups *and* the downs of relating to the opposite sex, people just as flawed and wounded as you are.

It should actually be of tremendous encouragement to realize that until you marry, nothing's final. Until you make a covenant before God and vow to cherish, honor, and serve another, God can use the process of dating and breaking up—sometimes *especially* breaking up—to refine and shape you.

If you have good reasons *not* to proceed towards marriage, a breakup is a blessing and godsend. But no matter how "right" it may be to end things, that ending often hurts. Breaking up with someone can raise questions about yourself and about the future.

When we began writing about dating relationships a couple of years ago, we had the privilege of talking to an insightful salesperson at a Christian bookstore. He said that many people who came in to buy a book about relationships were fresh from a breakup. Some came into the store with tear-stained faces. Some were ready to give up on the whole idea of dating. Yet some of these very people would come in the following Valentine's Day to purchase the latest book on dating for their new boyfriend or girlfriend.

This clerk had a hard time pointing singles who had experienced a breakup to the right material. What it seemed they really needed were words of healing and encouragement directed specifically to their situation. We hope that this chapter will provide some counsel and advice for those who have recently endured a breakup, as well as those who may undergo one in the future.

Just because a relationship comes to an end doesn't mean that you have failed or that you have missed your only chance at happiness. Rather, breaking up *well* gives you the opportunity to move forward in life with new insight, skill, and direction. And that's what this chapter is about.

CAN PEOPLE BREAK UP AND STAY FRIENDS?

This is often the biggest question on people's minds. People always seem to promise that they'll "stay close" or "remain friends," but does that ever *really* happen?

In a stereotypical breakup one person wants the relationship to end and tells the other person, who's totally shocked. This leads to a big fight that ends things. I (Jerusha) remember a breakup turning particularly sour. The guy actually stormed out of the restaurant without paying the bill and then kicked a trash can on his way out.

Anger, jealousy, and confusion are often a part of this kind of "conventional" breakup. *Just last week everything seemed to be perfect. Now we can't stand each other and things are over? How could this have happened?* The person who's being broken up with sometimes questions his self-worth and becomes uncertain about the future: *Do I have a chance with anyone else? Are the friends that we shared still going to be my friends?*

The pain hits home when you get your stuff back. A friend of ours had a box dropped on her driveway; the box contained all the special mementos of the relationship she'd been in for four years—hundreds of letters, keepsakes, and pictures. She cried as she looked through it, wondering, *Is this all that's left of the time I invested and all I gave of myself?*

Things can get even more bewildering when you doubt whether

things are *really* over. Maybe you end up kissing one more time, or you hear from friends that your ex misses you.

Every song on the radio seems to be about breaking up and speaks directly to *your* situation. Everywhere you go, you encounter special places you shared as a couple, and the sight of a restaurant you discovered together suddenly turns your heart inside out. If you happen to run into the other person, even for a brief moment, a queasy feeling in your stomach eats away at you.

To make matters worse, you have to retell the breakup story a hundred times. Everyone wants to know exactly what happened. At times, gossip makes the whole situation even more unbearable. People speculate about the whys and the hows. The person whom you thought cared so much about you says the worst possible things. Maybe you join in because you hurt so badly and you yourself want an outlet.

Is this what you're destined to experience when you break up?

This may be how some breakups happen, and it may be what we've come to consider normal, but a breakup doesn't have to be this way! It *is* possible to break up well and, yes, even to stay friends.

Rob and Carrie met (would you believe this?) in fifth grade. They didn't start dating until after their third year of high school, however. Via e-mail, Rob and Carrie shared with us their experience—from their first few interactions through their journey in learning to break up well.

Rob characterized the beginning of their relationship as "young, exciting, amazing…possibly foolish. I had no previous experience in a quality long-term relationship, and in hindsight I see that I really didn't know what I was getting myself into."

The two had dated for a full year. They both admit that they saw they needed to break up before they actually did. Carrie compared the situation to a storm on the horizon that neither wanted to acknowledge. Two major factors contributed to their breakup: They were moving apart geographically, and they had crossed both emotional and physical boundaries.

Rob and Carrie found that they *could* remain friends if they leaned on the Lord and allowed Him to guide their future interaction as well as shape their individual feelings. Here's how Rob describes the keys for moving on in the Lord's strength:

Make God number one… Forgive the other person if you need to. Then let all negative feelings go. I cannot stress enough the importance of dropping all bitterness that the heart might conjure up during this time. Chances are you'll *never* know the full reason for the breakup. Just understand that you need to move on and then allow God to mend the bridges that might have been burned.

Carrie also acknowledged God's part in enabling her and Rob to break up well.

Honestly, it has been God; I can't give credit anywhere else. When we started sharing about what God had been doing in our lives instead of focusing on the sadness of breaking up, things definitely seemed to get better. We also had to take some "breaks" from our friendship, times when we didn't have any contact. Those times were really hard, but it was good to take a step back and gain some perspective.

Rob and Carrie remain friends to this day, even though they are separated by thousands of miles now that Carrie lives in Calcutta, India, as a missionary. They reflect on their past relationship with thanks to God for teaching them through each other. Rob summed things up with this final comment:

Though we are not together anymore, I would not trade the world
for the loving friendship I gained with Carrie. God continues to
use her in my life to draw me closer to Him.

After hearing Rob and Carrie's story, we hope you're encouraged. But
you may also be asking how your relationship can come to the same end
that Rob and Carrie's did. How *do* you break up with grace, able to honor
God and the other person when the relationship ends?

THE FINAL DTR

There are obviously two sides to any breakup. In Rob and Carrie's case,
there was a mutual agreement to end things, but each of them had to deal
with their individual emotions and needs. Both felt the emotions of having been broken up with.

In many instances, there will be a more clear-cut assignment of roles:
Someone does the breaking up, and someone is broken up with. We're
going to examine, from both of these viewpoints, how to bring a relationship to a healthy end. Let's start with the person who's doing the
breaking up.

A good breakup starts with a good and final DTR. Yet even before
you talk, take some time to define the relationship on your own. Get on
your knees and pray. You need wisdom for this kind of conversation, and
the Lord is the only source for it. Ask God to guide you through the
details of the conversation. Also intercede for the other person. Ask God
to open her mind and heart to what He has for both of you. Bring her
needs before God. This time spent in prayer will gain you not only wisdom
but also tenderness and compassion for the person you're breaking up with.

If you are choosing to break up because you have been deeply
wounded—perhaps the person has slandered you or been unfaithful—

you *still* need to spend this time in prayer. In fact, we'd say that you need it more than ever! Beyond asking for wisdom and interceding for the other person, admit your own hurt before the Lord. Seek His healing and His comfort. He promises, "I will lead them and comfort those who mourn.... May they have peace...for I will heal them" (Isaiah 57:18-19, NLT). The God of all creation proclaims to you, "I, even I, am the one who comforts you" (Isaiah 51:12, NLT).

You also want to use this personal DTR to think through what has happened in the relationship and what went wrong. You'll want to be specific with your boyfriend or girlfriend, so during these moments you spend on your own with the Lord, outline your relationship. You can write things down if you think doing so will help you to be more articulate and communicate more effectively. You don't have to take these notes with you, but they will serve as a guide for your memory. That way you will be prepared to clearly define the problems and why you feel the way you do. This kind of open communication is the only way to truly honor the other person; it will help him understand the situation and your perspective.

Don't simply look at the negative during your personal DTR. Spend an equal amount of time thinking about the things you can affirm about this person and the time you spent with her. When you break up with someone, you may cause her to call into question her self-worth. So you should be prepared to support and encourage her as a child of God.

This may be difficult if you have been recently wounded, but there *were* reasons that you got into a relationship with this person. You can move forward in healing when you balance your perspective by recalling the good times you shared and the things that make that person unique and special.

When you have spent enough time in prayer and reflection to feel able both to confirm the person's worth and to communicate why you need to end the relationship, it's time to go to the person you've been dating.

We suggest at this point that you review the chapter "When to DTR." Take into account the different factors such as time of day, place, and time of life. It goes without saying that breaking up with someone right after his birthday party is not the most sensitive move in the world. And, as a final reminder, don't try to squeeze the DTR in between other things. Give yourself—and the other person—plenty of time to talk.

A breakup DTR should incorporate all the characteristics of healthy communication and loving responsiveness that we discussed previously. But a breakup requires some additional guidelines.

You must be honest about the issues at hand. Don't idealize or gloss over things, especially if they are areas of sin. If you know that you've stepped over the boundary lines physically, for instance, don't just say that you "need some time apart."

In your personal DTR, you sketched out specifics. It's time to share those. Define the problem as succinctly and carefully as possible. Separate the problem from the other person, no matter how easy it would be to affix blame. A healthy, godly breakup will never include an attack on the person. Even if the person you've been dating has done some nasty things to you, take the higher ground. In Romans 12:17, God charges us to "never pay back evil for evil to anyone" (NLT).

In humility, admit your own failings to the person you've dated and ask for forgiveness. You have probably done plenty of things wrong in the relationship. Ask for forgiveness for your missteps and inappropriate actions and decisions.

It's not always fitting to apologize for breaking up, however. Sometimes ending the relationship is exactly what you need to do. It can sound condescending, though, to ask for forgiveness for hurting a person by breaking up with him. Exercise discernment and wisdom as you choose your words.

Start and end the entire DTR with positives. In other words, sandwich the hard things you say between uplifting ones. Tell the person why you enjoyed dating her and identify the positives she brought to the relationship. Be sure to be honest, straightforward, and as clear as possible.

At this point (if not before!), be ready to hear the other person's side. He may or may not want to share what he is thinking and feeling. In any case, leave that door open and be willing to listen to whatever his perspective might be. If the breakup has come as a complete surprise to him, you may encounter hostility or tears or both. After all, he may not have had the benefit of either putting his thoughts and feelings in order or taking them before the Lord.

In responding to another person's anger or frustration, be gracious. A breakup should not be a bloodbath! Hang on to these words of Paul: "Let your conversation be gracious and effective so that you will have the right answer for everyone" (Colossians 4:6, NLT). Never slip into yelling or finger-pointing, no matter how heated the other person may get. Stay away from tit for tat. You don't have to have the final word, nor do you have to prove you're "right."

As 1 Peter 3:8 concludes, "Live in harmony with one another; be sympathetic, love as brothers, be compassionate and humble." Peter instructs us to be three things: sympathetic, compassionate, and humble. Following this advice is a great way to shape a breakup DTR. By extending sympathy, you share the other person's feelings. In compassion, you alleviate her suffering as much as you possibly can. And in humility, you display transparency and vulnerability. You refuse to let your pride dictate the way things go.

Finally, if you truly mean to end the relationship, do it. Be consistent and clear. Don't give mixed signals. "Let your 'Yes' be yes and your 'No,' no" (James 5:12). If you have prayed about it and are convinced that it's time to move on, don't string the person along with maybes, ifs, or whens.

With a breakup DTR like the one we just described, you are likely to remain friends. You've done nothing to dishonor the person or necessitate ultimate separation. Recognize, though, that this person will need space for healing. Don't underestimate the possibility that you might too. Although you may want to be friends, you will not immediately be close.

Breaking up with grace will have taught you to seek the Lord in prayer, communicate more effectively, and show respect for another person even during a difficult conversation. These are invaluable life lessons, and we pray that each of you would be so equipped.

The Deep End

Now what makes for a healthy breakup on the other end? What if someone's breaking up with you? First, remember that there is hope beyond breaking up, even though it doesn't always feel that way. Here are eight steps for moving through the loss.

1. Grieve the Loss

The first thing most people need to do is probably the hardest: Grieve. Now and then relationships end with pain playing a lesser part. For most people, though, a breakup, no matter how healthy, hurts. You can have peace about the Lord's will in separating you and agree that things should end, but you may still ache from the loss.

The depth and intensity of your relationship will determine the magnitude of your grief. Ending a serious relationship can be comparable to losing a loved one through death or divorce. Even ending a casual dating relationship can be painful.

Most of us would like to avoid all pain. But delaying suffering only intensifies the feelings once they surface. Also, don't try to shake things off by stuffing your emotions or masquerading behind a happy face.

The blessing of grief is that if you choose to enter into it, if you let yourself feel it and allow it to change you, God *will* bring comfort. He promises this in Matthew 5:4: "Blessed are those who mourn, for they *will* be comforted" (emphasis added). To find succor, you need to go through the sorrow.

Don't be afraid to cry. Sometimes you can't get everything out simply by talking it to death. Chuck Swindoll wrote, "When words fail, tears flow. Tears have a language all their own, a tongue that needs no interpreter. In some mysterious way, our complex inner-communication system knows when to admit its verbal limitations...and the tears come."[1] Tears help to unleash feelings that have been buried beneath the surface. Tears cleanse, heal, and renew.

And your tears matter to the Lord. David wrote, "You keep track of all my sorrows. You have collected all my tears in your bottle. You have recorded each one in your book" (Psalm 56:8, NLT). Eugene Peterson's translation of the same verse from Psalm 56 reads, "You've kept track of my every toss and turn through the sleepless nights, each tear entered in your ledger, each ache written in your book" (MSG). Each tear collected and recorded. Every toss and turn shared and noted. Every ache written in His book. Think of that.

I (Jerusha) like to imagine that all the tears God has collected in bottles will be waiting for us in heaven. I dream that we'll be able to take each of those sorrows and trade them for joy. Maybe we'll get to smash them in celebration like people smash dishes at Greek parties or Jewish weddings.

While you're grieving, you can also cling to these four words, which have helped us through countless periods of mourning: *This, too, shall pass.* Nothing lasts forever. Both bitter sorrow and sweet joy come and go. In *The Prison Chronicle,* Aleksandr Solzhenitsyn phrased this truth eloquently: "The bitter doesn't last forever and the sweet never fills the cup to overflowing."[2] As you grieve, seek and embrace the promises of comfort from God's Word. One of our favorite verses is Psalm 30:5: "Weeping may remain for a night, but rejoicing comes in the morning."

2. Get Out

Although you need to feel the pain of loss in order to receive the healing and comfort that come on the other side, don't isolate yourself in your sorrow. When we hurt, we often back off from fellowship, or we "fake it" around people so we don't have to let them into our ache. If we could only recognize that so many feel the same way we do, and at the same moment!

Closing all the blinds, sitting in bed with a tube of Pillsbury cookie dough, and watching *Sleepless in Seattle* may be all right for a day (we know that's what all you guys out there would do), but you cannot withdraw from life after a breakup.

The classic devotional *Streams in the Desert* shares this truth:

> Sorrow that is endured in the right spirit impacts our growth favorably.... Sitting down and brooding over our sorrow deepens the darkness surrounding us, allowing it to creep into our heart. And soon our strength has changed to weakness. But if we will turn from the gloom and remain faithful to the calling of God, the light will shine again and we will grow stronger.[3]

So get out and be with other people. Choose life. Hang out with friends who understand what you've been through but who don't need to gossip about it. Plan activities that will keep your mind occupied.

Do we need to point out that listening to "your song" or going to "your special places" is probably not the best idea? If possible, pick up something new with a friend. Try a dance class, go out and test drive some sports cars you've always admired, or go to one of those "make your own pottery" shops. Get involved with others in positive, constructive ways.

3. Focus on the Good Memories

A healthy response to breaking up involves choosing to remember the positive things that came out of the relationship.

Chuck Swindoll advises, "We're missing it—God's best—if the fun memories are being eclipsed by the fierce ones."[4] The Lord commands us to "fix [our] thoughts on what is true and honorable and right. Think about things that are pure and lovely and admirable. Think about things that are excellent and worthy of praise" (Philippians 4:8, NLT). God's best for you includes turning your thoughts away from the negative and focusing on the good.

Your pain will ease as you replay the joyful interactions you shared with the person you broke up with. It may take some training to focus on the positive aspects of your past relationship, but the reward—in the form of your peace and release—will be great.

Someone once claimed that a well-trained memory is one that permits you to forget everything that isn't worth remembering. We like that. God can train your memory, if you take every thought to Him (see 2 Corinthians 10:5). Ask Him to help you put out of your mind everything that's not worth recalling and to concentrate instead on what is worth remembering.

In saying that you should dwell on the positive aspects of your relationship, we don't want to trivialize or simplify the very real emotions of grief and hurt that come with many breakups. Sometimes when you're grieving, remembering the good things can bring another wave of sorrow. Yet choosing to be thankful for the times of joy you had, rather than completely dismissing the relationship because it ended with pain, will help you move forward.

4. Laugh

When you've come through the grief of loss, chosen to interact with others, and fixed your mind on the encouraging parts of the past, you're ready for the fourth healthy way to react to a breakup: laughter.

If you've just barely broken up with someone, laughing may be the last thing in the world you can picture yourself doing. But laughter is one of the most beautiful and beneficial therapies God granted humanity. In fact, the old adage that laughter is the best medicine has a lot of truth to it. Richard Foster wrote,

> Indeed, Norman Cousins in his book, *Anatomy of an Illness,* discusses how he used the therapy of laughter to help him overcome a crippling disease. In his hospital bed Cousins watched old Marx Brothers films and *Candid Camera* shows, and the genuine belly laughter he experienced seemed to have an anesthetic effect and gave him pain-free sleep. Doctors even confirmed the salutary effect of laughter on his body chemistry.[5]

Looking for the humor in life will go a long way in helping you move on after a breakup. Proverbs 15:15 tells us, "for the happy heart, life is a continual feast" (NLT). Wouldn't you rather be feasting on life than starving yourself on bitterness and resentment?

Keeping a good sense of humor is a great way to avoid irritability and heaviness of spirit: "A cheerful heart is good medicine, but a broken spirit saps a person's strength" (Proverbs 17:22, NLT). Laughing might come through reading the comics in the morning, watching a hilarious movie, interacting with a friend, or simply enjoying the serendipities of daily life.

Though it's a bit of a cliché, it's true that the happiest people in life don't necessarily have everything; they just make the best of everything.

Part of making the best of things is learning to laugh again. Laughter moves you forward and away from the breakup.

5. *Forgive*

The first four points we've shared with you are great ways to respond in a healthy, godly manner to a breakup. Yet someone who's serious about surviving a breakup will press on through four final steps. These are more challenging to the spirit, but they will bring greater maturity and a deeper sense of God's presence and blessing.

Forgiveness is the next step in surviving a breakup. When people break up poorly, you'll often find them expressing feelings of hatred or rage directed toward their ex. In an attempt to deal with their woundedness, they lash out against the person who they believe caused it all.

As a wise but unnamed person once said, "Hating people is like burning down your own house to get rid of a rat." Hatred does more harm to you than anyone else. Adolph Coors phrased it this way: "Hatred is like the barrel of a shotgun that's plugged. Pretty soon it's going to go off in your face. It hurts the hater more than the hated."[6] And Scripture warns of the devastating effects of acting out in hatred: "If ye bite and devour one another, take heed that ye be not consumed one of another" (Galatians 5:15, KJV).

If you choose to bite and devour your ex after a breakup, you will be destroyed by your hatred. The Lord commands us to "make allowance for each other's faults and forgive the person who offends you. Remember, the Lord forgave you, so you must forgive others" (Colossians 3:13, NLT).

We don't know what you've gone through in a breakup. It might have been something incredibly heartbreaking. It may have been something unbelievably agonizing. Perhaps you're thinking that there's no *way* you can forgive your ex.

God speaks clearly. He has forgiven you—for everything! Every wound you've inflicted on another person or yourself. Every time you've grieved Him. Every time you've chosen death instead of life. Because you have been forgiven, you must forgive others. There's no way around it.

Granting forgiveness to another person means surrendering your sense of being entitled to hurt the person who hurt you. It means submitting to God your felt right to avenge yourself.

And forgiveness goes beyond this. It also willingly relinquishes the rancor and the feelings of resentment that can accompany woundedness. Dwight Carlson wrote, "Forgiveness means that we actively choose to give up our grudge despite the severity of the injustice done to us." We *decide* not to hold on to the pain. Carlson continued, "It does not mean that we have to say or feel, 'That didn't hurt me' or 'It didn't really matter.' Some things may hurt very much, and we must not deny that fact, but after fully recognizing the hurt, we should choose to forgive."[7]

We experience the freedom to forgive not because we have forgotten what happened or denied the pain but *because* we have validated the hurt and *chosen* to turn it over to He who forgives. Lewis Smedes words it this way: "When you forgive someone for hurting you, you perform spiritual surgery inside your soul; you cut away the wrong that was done to you."[8] Just as a physical surgery repairs the damaged body, the spiritual surgery of forgiveness mends the injured soul.

Finally, forgiveness cleanses the mind, the heart, *and the mouth.* Ephesians 4:31-32 presents this great challenge: "Get rid of all bitterness, rage, anger, harsh words, and slander, as well as all types of malicious behavior. Instead, be kind to each other, tenderhearted, forgiving one another, just as God through Christ has forgiven you" (NLT).

6. *Avoid Gossip*

These verses from Ephesians take us to the next step in surviving a breakup. After we forgive, we must purge our lives of all "harsh words, and slander, as well as all types of malicious behavior." The Lord demands that we lay aside gossip after a breakup. We must not tear down a brother or sister who's ended a relationship with us. The direction from God's Word is crystal clear.

The obvious reason to avoid slander is that our words would hurt the other person. But consider for a moment what gossip does to *you*. Chuck Swindoll tells the story of a young boy growing up in the Swiss Alps with his grandfather. The boy loved to hear his voice echo across the mountains and would often call out "I LOVE YOU." Back his sentiments would come "I LOVE YOU, I love you, I love you, love you, love you…"

One day, however, the grandfather was forced to discipline the little boy, who had been extremely naughty. In his rebellious anger, the young boy shouted at his grandfather, "I HATE YOU!" To his shock and dismay, the words bounced back and hit him: "I HATE YOU, I hate you, I hate you, hate you, hate you." The boy felt his own hatred. It stung him as much as, if not more than, it did his grandfather.

Swindoll calls this the law of echoes: What we say comes back to us.[9] How we talk about a person after a breakup will impact us. Our slander will come back to bite and devour. In Proverbs we read, "What dainty morsels rumors are—but they sink deep into one's heart" (Proverbs 18:8; 26:22, NLT). Even the smallest of words spoken in bitterness against an ex will descend into your own soul.

After breaking up with someone, remember the law of echoes. Recognize that gossip wounds not only the other person, but also yourself.

A final note: If the person you broke up with engages in gossip, you must still choose to get rid of harsh words in obedience to the Lord's commands. Although the other person may be picking fights with you through slander, *your* choice to put an end to gossip will quiet his tongue. Proverbs 26:20 promises, "Fire goes out for lack of fuel, and quarrels disappear when gossip stops" (NLT).

7. Learn from God in the Storm

By now you've reached the point where you are ready to see what God can teach you through the pain of your breakup. After all, God "displays his power in the whirlwind and the storm" (Nahum 1:3, NLT). You've just gone through a whirlwind and a storm. Now it's time to look for God's mighty demonstration of power.

When a breakup occurs, it's natural to question what God intended by it, as well as what He plans for your future. Perhaps you feel betrayed by God because this relationship was something you dearly desired. We'd like to share with you the following poem, which beautifully describes God's design even in disappointments:

> Is there some door closed by the Father's hand
> Which widely opened you had hoped to see?
> Trust God and wait—for when He shuts the door
> He keeps the key.
>
> Is there some earnest prayer unanswered yet,
> Or answered NOT as you had thought 'twould be?
> God will make clear His purpose by and by.
> He keeps the key.
>
> Have patience with your God, your patient God,
> All wise, all knowing, no long lingerer He,
> And of the door of all your future life
> He keeps the key.
>
> Unfailing comfort, sweet and blessed rest,
> To know if EVERY door He keeps the key
> That He at last, when just HE sees best,
> Will give it thee.
>
> —Anonymous

What we *know* to be true, what we choose to believe in faith, is that God is in control. The Word proclaims that "God…is the blessed controller of all things, the king over all kings and the master of all masters" (1 Timothy 6:15, Phillips).

Whether you are dating or breaking up, *nothing* falls outside of God's perfect sovereignty. No matter how out of control a breakup *feels,* you can trust in the biblical assurance that God is the blessed controller.

You can also cling to the two-edged truth that nothing can separate you from God and that you will conquer through His love. As Romans 8:35,37 declares, "Who shall separate us from the love of Christ? Shall trouble or hardship or persecution or famine or nakedness or danger or sword?… No, in all these things we are more than conquerors through him who loved us."

The trouble and hardship of a breakup are not beyond God's control, nor is it beyond His power to help you become a conqueror through them. God, the blessed controller, will not be separated from you!

We also affirm the biblical truth that God Himself does not allow adversity in order to harm you. As the prophet Jeremiah wrote ages ago, "Though he brings grief, he will show compassion, so great is his unfailing love. *For he does not willingly bring affliction or grief to the children of men*" (Lamentations 3:32-33, emphasis added). As Jerry Bridges wrote,

Every adversity that comes across our path, whether large or small, is intended to help us grow in some way. If it were not beneficial, God would not allow it or send it, "For he does not willingly bring affliction or grief to the children of men." God does not delight in our sufferings. He brings only that which is necessary, but He does not shrink from that which will help us grow.[10]

Sometimes the very thing we'd like to evade—pain—can teach us the greatest lessons. Oswald Chambers further emphasizes this truth:

> When God gets us alone through suffering, heartbreak, temptation, disappointment, sickness, or by thwarted desires, a broken friendship…when He gets us absolutely alone, and we are totally speechless, unable to ask even one question, *then* He begins to teach us.[11]

God has gotten you alone with Him. Heartbreak, or at least a broken friendship, has left you standing before Him. Now is the time to seek Him to find out what He wants to teach you.

God has good in store for you after a breakup. We love the sweet truth He unveils in Jeremiah 32:41: "I will rejoice in doing them good and will assuredly plant them in this land with all my heart and soul." All of God's heart and soul delights in doing *you* good. He will soon plant you in the land with a new vision for His way and a renewed trust in His control.

Finally, remember that God will not abandon you. You have His promise and David's testimony: "Those who know your name will trust in you, for you, LORD, have never forsaken those who seek you" (Psalm 9:10).

8. Comfort Others

As you have progressed through each step of your breakup experience, you've experienced and been uplifted by God's comfort for you. Now He asks you to extend that comfort to others.

There's nothing quite so healing as helping another in need. George Matheson, Scottish preacher, author, and composer of hymns, once wrote, "He is best indeed who learns to make the joy of others cure his own heartache."

Part of God's perfect design for comfort is that as we receive, we become equipped to give. He fills us and enables us to then meet others in need. We read in 2 Corinthians 1:3-4, "All praise to the God and Father of our Lord Jesus Christ. He is the source of every mercy and the God who comforts us. He comforts us in all our troubles so that we can comfort others. When others are troubled, we will be able to give them the same comfort God has given us" (NLT).

Of course, it might be easier to avoid sharing our pain with others. We wouldn't have to relive any of the hurtful memories or think about the past at all. Indeed,

> Many of us could…deal with our grief if only we were allowed to
> do so in private. Yet what is so difficult is that most of us are called
> to exercise our patience not in bed but in the open street, for all to
> see. We are called upon to bury our sorrows, not in restful inactiv-
> ity, but in active service—contributing to other people's joy.[12]

When you choose to serve God by comforting others with the comfort He's given you, you will receive from Him amazing blessing.

This is the final step to surviving a breakup, not only because you simply could not comfort others without going through the first seven steps, but also because it launches you into the future. You have survived a breakup. You can now be a minister to others.

Many people will suffer from and in broken relationships. You have been divinely appointed to offer comfort to these hurting ones as God places them in your life. Go forward now, equipped by the God and Father of our Lord Jesus!

When a DTR Helps You Not to Communicate

Derek was relieved to meet someone he could have fun with and be himself around. The first month after transferring to a new city had been agony for him—full of many failed attempts to build relationships with people who were too attached to their own clique to notice those who had just arrived. Janice, though, seemed easygoing, smart, and comfortable to be with, and he thought she was probably a strong Christian.

For a few months, Derek and Janice interacted mainly in group settings, but eventually they began getting together as a twosome. They started to go out on dates, and things went well for them.

About a month into their dating relationship, Janice began to talk with Derek about her past. Derek was shocked and hurt to find out that Janice had only recently broken up with a longtime boyfriend back home. It only made matters worse when she explained in great detail about the physical boundaries they had crossed.

But Derek assumed that to honor Janice and show her that he trusted her as much as she did him, he needed to tell her about his past sins too. The two spent long nights going over their family dynamics, previous relationships, and the mistakes they had made.

Derek wanted us to know that he did try to steer their relationship in godly ways. A mentor of his had talked with him about relationships on numerous occasions. Two of the key things they discussed were "guarding the heart" and accountability.

Derek had always known that he needed buddies to keep him accountable, but after he met Janice, he spent most of his time either alone with her or in groups, so he didn't have very deep guy friendships. And after those long talks late at night and early into the morning, he felt bonded to Janice in a way he couldn't explain. Someone *knew* him for the first time in a long while, and it felt good.

Five months into their relationship, Janice started demanding that Derek take her everywhere with him. If he wanted to shoot hoops with the guys, she had to be there. If he was going to watch a movie with some guy friends, she'd show up—invited or not. She began expressing jealous and hostile feelings toward Derek's other relationships. Derek cared deeply about Janice and wanted her to be happy, so he didn't bring up his frustrations.

At this point Janice revealed even more of her past, including the fact that she had been abused as a child. Derek's heart ached for her, and he yearned to rescue her from the pain and fear she still felt. He thought that as her boyfriend, as her *friend,* he should try to counsel her and help her as best he could. He felt as if he could help her if he loved her enough.

Remarkably, their relationship did start to get better. Janice moved in with a godly roommate and seemed less focused on the hurts of her past. She also grew more interested in talking about spiritual matters. She threw herself into service at the church and volunteered for an upcoming missions trip to Guatemala. When Janice's financial support didn't come in on time, Derek offered to pay for her trip.

About this time things went south for Derek. He got into a four-car wreck (his fault), and he had to leave the church where he was serving because of some conflicts with other staff members. Derek sought comfort in Janice, but she seemed unable or unwilling to be there for him.

Janice left on her missions trip shortly thereafter, and Derek had two weeks to evaluate their relationship and seek counsel. He talked at length with a godly couple he knew from church, and they gave him some sound advice. He reaffirmed in his heart that he wanted to reorder his relationship with Janice to more fully glorify the Lord.

But Janice came back from the missions trip with a different attitude. She had met someone. She was *really* in love now. She couldn't see Derek anymore. Not at all.

Heartbroken and confused, Derek tried to sort through the past year and look at all that had happened. He felt as if someone had turned him inside out and everyone could see the depths of his anguish. He felt violated and exposed. He didn't think he could trust anyone with his heart ever again. Guard his heart now? It seemed like a joke. There was nothing left to guard.

EMOTIONAL PROMISCUITY

It may seem odd in a book on DTRs—communication—to discuss ways and reasons *not* to communicate, but in order for your intentional conversations with your date to be most effective, you need to keep in mind what might be *too* far to go.

Derek and Janice were what we would call "emotionally promiscuous." They shared with each other on an emotional level, which led them to a deeper intimacy than their relationship could handle. This resulted in heartbreak and feelings of betrayal when they stopped seeing each other romantically.

In another book, we define sexual promiscuity as "any haphazard or thoughtless sexual behavior. It could be failing to decide your sexual standards ahead of time. It could include doing 'whatever feels right.'"[1] Emotional promiscuity, then, can be any haphazard or thoughtless *emotional* behavior. It can be failing to decide your boundaries ahead of time. It can mean doing "whatever feels right." You can be emotionally promiscuous just as easily as you can be sexually promiscuous.

Peter tells us "your enemy the devil prowls around like a roaring lion looking for someone to devour" (1 Peter 5:8). One of the primary temptations he dangles before singles is to compromise their physical boundaries. Yet we've seen a subtle change in the Enemy's focus. He's already won ground on the battlefield of sexual temptation, but he's not satisfied with that. He wants the heart, not just the body. So he has devised a more insidious method: tempting single Christians into believing that they don't need to guard their emotional purity as zealously as they guard their physical purity.

As a Christian community, we have failed to recognize the intensity of the Enemy's effort to tempt singles into emotional promiscuity. We may hear a token talk on Proverbs 4:23, "Guard your heart, for it is the wellspring of life," but some churches don't even go this far. I (Jerusha) didn't learn about the concept of guarding my heart until halfway through college. Looking back at my dating history, I think I would have greatly benefited from someone discussing with me the dangers of emotional promiscuity.

But it is difficult to nail down the specifics of guarding the heart. Furthermore, we often come up against the general consensus that it's healthy and right to share your heart with the person you are dating.

While we do not completely disagree with this consensus, we believe strongly that godly boundaries must be set for the level of emotional intimacy on which a couple relates before marriage. Just as two people can prematurely give their bodies to each other, they can also give their spirits and hearts to each other before they are ready. Derek, for example, had given so much of himself—and had taken so much of Janice—that he felt they were emotionally "one." This made the severing of the relationship extremely painful.

Many Christian couples substitute emotional intimacy for physical intimacy. They can't "go all the way" physically, so they "go all the way" emotionally instead, giving all of themselves on a level that seems less dangerous.

The perils of emotional promiscuity are very real. And you encounter those dangers even if you don't share about your past sins as Derek and Janice did. You have an inner heart—a place of hopes and dreams, passions and fears—that belongs only to the Lord and your mate, if He chooses to give you one. He *has* commanded you to guard this heart, for it is the wellspring of life. You need to earnestly protect this sacred place. You need to guard your emotional purity as ardently as you do your physical purity.

It takes great restraint to enter marriage physically and emotionally chaste. George Sala once said that restraint is learning "not only to say the right thing in the right place, but far more difficult, to leave unsaid the wrong thing at the tempting moment." Staying emotionally chaste begins with learning to control your tongue. In James we read, "If anyone is never at fault in what he says, he is a perfect man, able to keep his whole body in check.... The tongue also is a fire, a world of evil among the parts of the body. It corrupts the whole person, sets the whole course of his life on fire, and is itself set on fire by hell" (James 3:2,6).

Don't we *wish* we could learn to control the tongue? But this is more than an incredibly difficult thing to do; it is humanly *im*possible. We have to dig deeper than self-help techniques and worldly wisdom if we are to stay emotionally chaste. We need the self-control, patience, and wisdom that only God can give.

Where to Find Wisdom

Wisdom tops the charts of the resources we need if we are to stay emotionally chaste. We turn again to the book of James, where we find this great encouragement: "If any of you lacks wisdom, he should ask God, who gives generously to all without finding fault, and it will be given to him" (1:5). The only responsibility we have is to ask God for wisdom, to "ask boldly, believingly, without a second thought" (1:6, MSG). We don't have to wonder whether God will grant the wisdom we need to remain emotionally pure. God offers wisdom graciously and abundantly. The Father "loves to help" (1:5, MSG), and He does so "without finding fault" (NIV) and "without making [us] feel foolish or guilty" (Phillips).

God alone is all-wise, the source of true guidance and hope. Turn to Him in prayer when you don't know what you're doing, when you have no clue how to rein in your tongue, and when you can't figure out how you should guard your heart.

A God-Controlled Self

The term *self-control* can be a bit deceiving. Can we humans truly control ourselves? Maybe for a while, but ultimately we will fail in any attempt to rule our own world. We will also fail to control how we talk and what we do in a relationship to avoid emotional promiscuity.

We say this not to discourage you but to release you! If you try to run your own show, you'll become frustrated and might give up. Genuine self-control comes only from the Holy Spirit. In essence, you are ruled by the Spirit when you refrain from words or acts that would prematurely bond you emotionally to someone. That restraint is evidence that you are not a "you-controlled self," but a "God-controlled self."

Sometimes becoming God-controlled boils down to simple timing. Learning to be a God-controlled self often translates into waiting to speak and waiting to act. Proverbs 13:3 proves this truth: "Those who control their tongue will have a long life; a quick retort can ruin everything" (NLT).

First Peter 1:13 commands, "Therefore, prepare your minds for action; be self-controlled." We need to *train* ourselves for right action because we're not born disciplined. We must prepare. This truth is crucial to the exercise of emotional restraint in a relationship. Learning now to be a God-controlled self will help you consider the timing of your words and your actions in relationships.

We also exercise self-control when we refrain from trying to influence others to like us. The reason most people become emotionally attached prematurely is that they are eager to be affirmed and validated as people. We do things to bond a person to ourselves because it makes us feel good, safe, and secure; we say things to hook another's emotions because we're concerned what she might think about us if we revealed who or what we *really* are.

Richard Foster wrote,

> The tongue is our most powerful weapon of manipulation. A frantic stream of words flows from us because we are in a constant process of adjusting our public image. We fear so deeply what we think people see in us that we talk in order to straighten out their understanding.[2]

Allow God to control your actions and your words. Don't speak hastily or in order to manipulate the emotions of another. Restraint will both display the fruit of God's Spirit—self-control—and guard you emotionally.

Sweet Fruit

To bring both wisdom and self-control together, we need patience. Like self-control, patience is a matter of timing, but it also relates to attitude. Patience translates into a state of being that's content to wait. Patience means trusting that holding off in a relationship is not only the *right* thing to do, but also the *best* thing to do.

Someone once said that patience is bitter but its fruit is sweet. And how far sweeter is the fruit of God-given patience than any sense of sweet satisfaction we may gain from bonding with a person before it's time!

If we want to know what God has in store for us, we must wait for Him to arrange the details. Hebrews 10:36 confirms, "Patient endurance is what you need now, so you will continue to do God's will. Then you will receive all that he has promised" (NLT). God has plans in store for your emotional fulfillment. You need patience to wait for Him to reveal those in His time.

I (Jerusha) have often joked that patience is not one of my strongest virtues. I used to think this was because I just hadn't been given a whole lot to begin with. *Maybe God wants me to pray for more,* I reflected. Then I read this brief story about the renowned pianist Ignacy Paderewski. When he was quite old, Paderewski was approached by a fan who asked, "Is it true that you still practice every day?"

"Yes," he answered, "at least six hours."

Awestruck, the fan pointed out what she thought was obvious: "You must have a *world* of patience." To this the wise and seasoned Paderewski replied, "I have no more patience than the next fellow. I just use mine."

You may not feel you have enough patience to wait for God's timing for your emotional fulfillment. You're in a relationship *now* where you yearn to share yourself deeply and completely. To you we write this encouragement: Use what patience you have. God will supply the difference if you ask Him.

EMOTIONAL PACING

So how do wisdom, self-control, and patience play out in the day-to-day development of a relationship? How do you exercise these three God-given virtues?

First, you learn to pace relationships. When I (Jeramy) was about ten years old, my Aunt Lynette thought it would be a great idea to get me involved in a sport. An incredibly active and athletic young woman, she chose track and field for me because she thought I had natural speed and ability. Without conditioning or training me, Aunt Lynette entered me in my first race: a four-hundred-meter dash. Maybe she assumed I would practice on my own. Who knows?

The four-hundred-meter dash takes runners around the track one time. Looking over what seemed such a short distance, I confidently placed myself on the starting block and anticipated the taste of victory. (What is it about ten-year-old boys that causes *all of them* to assume they're going to win?)

The gun sounded and I took off, grabbing a quick lead. It felt so good. Looking down the track, no one stood between me and the finish line. I ran as fast as I could run.

But after about one hundred meters, my side started to ache, and breathing became difficult. I began to slow down. Realizing a few seconds later that I still had half the track to cover, I did a somersault onto the grass.

When you run, you have to pace yourself carefully, based on the kind of race you're in and the course you're on. Likewise, when you relate to a person of the opposite sex, you must pace your relationship emotionally.

Pacing a relationship means keeping an even stride. Since you are running with another person, pacing also involves staying in step with the person you're dating. If you don't pace a relationship, you'll end up like Jeramy—somersaulting into the sidelines.

Conditioning

It's important to view your relationship as if it is a long run, even a marathon. Whether or not you stay in a particular dating relationship for an extended period of time, never plan to "sprint" emotionally, revealing yourself in a dash and asking the other person to do the same.

You must also do some pre-race preparation, some conditioning. You've already begun conditioning by pursuing information about dating. Continuing to seek and acquire all the wisdom you can about interacting with the opposite sex will help you hone your tools for achieving and maintaining emotional balance.

But runners don't only prepare their minds. They also condition their bodies, getting each muscle ready for the strain ahead. You cannot neglect the conditioning of your emotional muscles: your heart and spirit. You can prepare yourself spiritually by committing to prayer, to the study of God's Word, to worship, to fellowship with other believers, and to serving the Lord in the ways He's created you to minister.

Before you enter the race, you also need to know what condition your heart is in, and you may need to get it in better condition. Many people enter relationships thinking they will satisfy their deep needs for affirmation and companionship. A great British mystery writer and Christian, P. D. James eloquently illustrates this phenomenon in her book *Death in Holy Orders*. One of the primary characters, Raphael, confesses to his professor not only his love for her, but also the hopes he held for what her returned love might mean:

> "It's just that I thought if I could make you like me—or perhaps even love me a little—I wouldn't be in such a muddle. Everything would be all right."
>
> She said more kindly, "But it wouldn't. If life is a muddle we can't look for love to make it all come right."

"But people do."...

[She stops and ponders.]... But if things were going wrong
for him—and she thought they were—what use was it looking
to someone else to put them right?[3]

Too often we look to others to "put right" the muddle of our life. But
others cannot bear the weight of our emotional needs. Biographer Alexander Whyte called this the human tendency to "hang very heavy weights
on very thin wires." We need to stop hanging the weight of our emotions
and spirits on the "thin wires" of other people.

Another part of conditioning yourself for healthy relationships is dealing with any emotional baggage that may weigh down a relationship.
Each of us has needs and faces different spiritual and emotional challenges. Some of us may need more help than others to experience freedom
from emotional weight. If you are dealing with a lot of emotional weight,
you may want to pursue meeting with someone who can pray with you
and counsel you. If a layperson seems unqualified to process the particular concerns of your heart, look to professional counselors, who can be
used mightily by God to help you bear and even unload your burdens.

Strategy

Once people condition their body in preparation for running, they devise
a strategy for how they will accomplish the specific goals they have set for
themselves. The person who plans to run a marathon trains differently
from someone who runs no more than a mile or two a day. People *plan* in
order to meet their goals. You, too, need to formulate a strategy for how
to emotionally pace a relationship.

The challenge is that no one can tell you exactly when to share things
or how to conduct yourself in order to protect both your own heart and
the heart of the person you're dating. The pace of a relationship depends

on so many factors: the maturity of the people involved, their stage of life, their expectations, and their desires.

We can't tell you that after a month you can share x, y, and z; or that on your year anniversary, you can start to talk about "these" things, share "these" emotions, or "do these" emotionally bonding activities. What we *can* tell you to do is to evaluate the factors that will determine the appropriate level of emotional intimacy for your relationship.

First, assess your maturity level. Are you able to discuss heavy topics with dignity and respect, or do you find yourself embarrassed and unnerved by such conversation?

Also consider what stage of life you are in right now. Are you ready for the emotional intensity of a serious relationship, or are there things in your life—career, school, family—that take priority for you or that would hinder the development of a relationship? For instance, an early college relationship should be significantly more guarded and proceed at a much slower pace than a relationship between two singles who would like to determine within a matter of months whether they will pursue marriage.

If you're not planning to get married soon, plan and pace yourself for a much longer emotional run. Imagine your relationship taking off at lightning pace so that you become closer to the person you're dating than you have ever been to anyone else. What if you break up? We refer to a breakup like this as a minidivorce because the couple has shared intimacies with each other that they haven't shared with any other. That is, they've been "married" in their hearts. So after they separate, they have to sever those bonds. Pacing your relationship at the right emotional level and speed will keep you from having to "divorce" your heart from another person.

We can also advise you to think *before* you say and do things. Start noticing the ways your words and actions impact others emotionally. Begin looking at the way other people's speech and conduct affect you.

These observations will help you realize how essential it is for you to stop before you speak and think before you act.

Finally, the emotional pace of your relationship should match the stage of your relationship. When you date casually, you begin at a slow pace, revealing and unveiling cautiously. During more serious and then exclusive dating, the pace quickens some because more information is needed to discern whether the relationship should continue. With engagement, the emotional pace picks up significantly—partners need to become transparent enough to prepare for marriage.

Vital Signs

The key to maintaining the right pace for any relationship is to constantly check the vital signs. Runners do this periodically, either on their own or by using belts and other devices to monitor their heart rate, breathing, and blood pressure. You check the vital signs of a relationship through self-evaluation and the input of others.

Taking the vital signs of your relationship involves looking objectively at what your conversations are about and how those topics seem to affect your interaction and emotional bond. If you take a moment to analyze what your talks center on, you may recognize that you need to exercise more restraint in what you say and when you say it. You may also realize that it's time to stop talking so much.

Proverbs 10:19 advises, "Don't talk so much. You keep putting your foot in your mouth. Be sensible and turn off the flow!" (TLB). Take periodic breaks from intense conversation in order to keep your pace appropriate, to guard the person you're dating, and to protect yourself.

Checking the vital signs of your relationship should help you determine if you're allowing emotional attachments to get in the way of healthy interaction. If you find you can't breathe in a relationship because of its emotional weightiness, then it's time to slow down just as a runner would to regain breath control. If you discover your relationship "blood pressure" skyrockets every time you do ——— or say something like ———, take steps to avoid such stress factors.

As you observe and assess, adjust your pace to avoid relational burnout. Most of the time, this adjustment means slowing things down. We tend to get ahead of ourselves in relationships far more often than we get behind.

But there *will* be times when a couple takes the vital signs of their relationship and realizes that they need to increase their pace because of where they are. Again, discerning where *your* individual relationship is will be a matter of exercising the wisdom, self-control, and patience that God provides and that we discussed earlier.

Pacing your relationship emotionally is essential to maintaining purity. It requires a lot to condition your heart and spirit and then monitor your emotional levels, but the effort will prove a worthwhile pursuit when you enter marriage or move on to another season in life free of the baggage of past attachments to others.

EMOTIONAL FLASHING AND OTHER DANGERS

In addition to pacing a relationship appropriately, you can take other steps to preserve emotional purity.

First, be aware that **honesty can result in inappropriate intimacy.** Being truthful does not equate to baring your soul. It *is* essential that you uphold a standard of honesty about and within your relationship. It's never appropriate to lie, gloss over, or cover up the truth even in order to "protect" someone.

However, you can be truthful to a fault. A prime example of this occurs when people reveal their "past sins" to each other. You do not need to share every detail and emotion from former relationships. This sometimes (often!) leads to more sin.

Look back at Derek and Janice's relationship. Talking about their previous physical mistakes did more damage to their relationship than good. It both awakened greater desire for inappropriate verbal and physical expression and bonded them to each other in a "no one else knows this secret about me" way.

Personal issues such as abuse, struggles with a particular sin, perhaps even something as difficult as rape or pregnancy may eventually need to be revealed to a person you are considering marrying. But being "honest" about these things with any date or friend of the opposite sex can set you up for an unhealthy emotional attachment.

We are wired to want to comfort others and even to redeem their pain. Being too honest with someone can prompt in that person a desire to save or rescue or fix. Humans cannot save one another. Both the person who's been "brutally honest" and the person he's shared with can experience serious disappointment and heartache when his expectations of emotional healing or fulfillment aren't met.

Second, **stay away from emotional flashing (and emotional flashers)**. Our good friend and fellow minister Darren Prince defined *emotional flashing* for us as "the sudden and brief display of a deep and private feeling or experience for the purpose of getting an emotional need met." This inappropriate revealing can be a quest for attention, for a sense of importance, or for comfort from the person listening. Emotional flashing can appear to be used for shock value, but the true motive usually has more to do with questions of security, acceptance, and validation.

An emotional flasher often wonders, *If I reveal ———— about myself, will I still be safe with this person? Will she still like me and approve of me? Will she be able to meet my needs after I make myself vulnerable?*

An example of emotional flashing is saying "I love you" before the relationship has reached the point of authentic love. Instead of expressing a genuine sentiment, this kind of emotional flashing is actually the unspoken question, Am I lovable?

In order to keep a relationship emotionally appropriate and healthy, you need to avoid flashing your emotions, and you also need to disengage from those who emotionally flash you on a regular basis. If you notice this becoming a pattern with a friend or date, you should talk to him first and see if the behavior changes. If it doesn't, you may need to step back from your established level of intimacy.

Inappropriately shared intimacies become hooks that ensnare a person. You "hook" a person by sharing with her or "flashing" her something she cannot ignore or escape. A healthy relationship does not want partners to be "hooked" to each other; they should be free. Free people are capable of choosing to join together or break apart. "Hooked" people are trapped in premature emotional intensity.

Sometimes a person who's been "too honest" *wants* to hook another. This is an unhealthy means of establishing security. If you recognize this tendency in a person you're dating, you can extract yourself from the web of hooks by taking some time apart and separating your own thoughts and feelings from the ideas and emotions of the other person. But don't stop there. Pray for a way to graciously speak about the matter and to encourage emotional health in that person.

Third, **know and respect your date's emotional limits.** You may feel comfortable sharing about certain things because they have no emotional intensity for you. For instance, talking about whether your kids should carry on the family tradition of names and titles might be a matter of course for you. It's something you'll eventually have to decide, and it doesn't hurt to get as many opinions as possible. But for someone else, this topic may indicate that you want to decide *with him.*

Just as you do in your physical relationship, you always need to defer to the person who has the stronger convictions about what should be expressed and when. You can also modify your emotional boundaries if one person feels that emotionally charged actions—such as the giving of expensive gifts or the celebration of particular events like anniversaries—must be undertaken or received in a certain way.

The person you're dating may be more emotionally cautious than you. Perhaps she's just gotten out of or over another relationship. Maybe the emotional scars of the past are still painful. Or perhaps she's watched others become too emotionally involved and has set some strong guidelines for herself based on what she's observed. Whatever the scenario, be aware and respectful of the convictions of anyone you date. You can also use the opportunity to evaluate whether your standards are set high enough.

Along a similar vein, **take into account that men and women differ in their emotional makeup.** It's amazing how much time, energy, and money we've invested in spreading the news that men and women aren't the same and don't think the same. From the age-old sugar and spice and everything nice versus snails and puppy-dog tails, to the modern Mars and Venus madness or the microwaves and Crockpot discussion, people always seem to be reiterating the simple truth that men and women are *different*. I think it's safe to say, "We get it!"

This basic difference between men and women contributes to the emotional health of a relationship by calling us to be sensitive to the fact that women can more easily become attached than men. Some experts suggest that this is because women use both sides of their brain, thus processing everything on the level of feeling as well as thought.

If you're this kind of woman, you probably require a stronger emotional guardedness during dating. If you're a man dating this kind of woman, you need to know and respect her sensitivity. But beware: There are women who are *not* wired in this manner, so men, don't treat every woman the same!

Taking into account how men and women differ also means recognizing that some men require less conversation than a woman might need to feel close to a person. Men may share sporadically, if at all, yet still sense a deep emotional bond. It's not the number of words that count but the content and nature of those words.

Here's another example of the different ways men and women approach relationships: Women can manipulate or force emotional intimacy in an attempt to get what they want from a man. Very rarely will a man initiate a night of passionate conversation. But women who want to be emotionally close (after all, it does feel good to them) may try to create such a night of revelation and then assume that the intimate conversation takes the relationship to the next level.

Women, the information that a man shares with you or allows you to share with him does not indicate the level of his commitment to you or his feelings for you. Men, if a woman tries to force emotional closeness, stand firm just as you would if she came on to you sexually.

We cannot highlight here all of the ways men and women differ, but it's safe to say that being alert to potential differences will help keep your relationship more emotionally pure.[4]

Finally, **don't trade emotional intimacy for physical intimacy.** Christians especially need to heed this warning. Believers know that they should not engage in sex before marriage, so they guard themselves against that "terrible sin." Yet many never consider the necessity of preserving emotional chastity.

We hear single Christians make comments like, "Our relationship's so great. We stay up all night talking, but nothing *physical* ever happens." Yet some of these couples may find that they are no better off than a couple who does make out all night. Christians are deceived if they think that a relationship built on premature emotional closeness leads to anything less than deep scarring. Dr. Gregg Jantz wrote,

> We are wrong…if we think that filling an emotional need is not as powerful a motivation as filling a physical one. We are physical beings, yes, but we are also highly emotional ones. For some men and most women, the fulfillment of emotional needs is paramount to the filling of physical ones.[5]

Just because you avoid sexual immorality doesn't mean you've chosen a healthy path for your relationship. The emotional bonds you forge by sharing too much too soon can leave deep wounds when a relationship ends. Many times it's harder to get over the loss of emotional intimacy than it is to overcome the purely physical memories. Why? Because the need to fill emotional needs is greater than the need to meet physical needs.

Christians can even use praying together as a way to bond emotion-ally. If you couch personal needs as prayer requests, it seems safe and even godly to share them and then pray about them with the person you're dat-ing. Yet when you're *supposedly* revealing your most intimate needs to God but *really* speaking so that the other person will hear, you're dishonoring the Lord, the person you're dating, and yourself.

Praying with another person is one of the most intimate and precious activities God allows us to share. Because of this, Christian couples should refrain from inappropriately engaging in extended one-on-one prayer time just as they should guard against the up-all-night-talking intimacy that seems so innocent.

Building a relationship that honors the Lord with emotional purity and guards each of the people involved requires a great deal of awareness, attention, and thought. We pray that reading this chapter has heightened your awareness of these issues, focused your attention on your role in a relationship, and stimulated your mind to consider your next moves.

As you learn to employ God-given wisdom, self-control, and patience to pace a relationship and set emotional boundaries, you will develop the capacity to remain emotionally chaste. You will be guarding your heart, the wellspring of your life, just as the Lord commanded. What an awesome gift to present to your Savior and your future spouse—a heart kept for them alone.

The Lowdown on Sex

The smell of freshly cut grass wafts through the evening air. The score-boards are tested in anticipation of the game that night. Somewhere in the distance, the "hut," "hike," and grunts of sixtysome athletes mix with the chanting voices of practicing cheerleaders. And busy at work are the field keepers, chalking the one-hundred-yard turf.

Each week field keepers mark the lines that indicate out of bounds, ten-yard increments, the midpoint at fifty yards, and the end zones. Maintaining a well-groomed field facilitates clear-cut play. It keeps players accountable to the rules of the game established long ago. And it grants them the freedom to play without wondering if they're where they're not supposed to be.

But after every game the chalk lines are blurred. Week after week, the field keepers come back to redraw the lines. What if they didn't? What if they expected the players to remember where the lines were last week?

God created a field for appropriate sexual conduct long before football was around. He established the rules, the limitations, and the way to emerge victorious. He defined how players in the game of life can stay within those limitations and enjoy the freedoms of sexual purity. And He's asking you to stay within the lines He's drawn for you.

But just as the play of two football teams eradicates the chalked lines laid out before each match, the play of day-to-day life can wear down the clearly marked boundaries of appropriate sexual desire and behavior. It's time for us all to rechalk the lines if we are going to be sexually pure.

STOKING THE FIRE

To define a relationship so that it pleases God and to clearly define the boundary lines He has drawn for you, you must cling to His grand view of sex and marriage. God could have created genderless, asexual beings instead of humankind. Yet He chose to pattern people after Himself: "Male and female he created them" (Genesis 1:27). We are sexual beings— and He called His creation "very good" (Genesis 1:31).

God celebrated the joining of the sexes in the first marriage. The male and female He created became one, and that too was very good (see Genesis 2:24). God made no mistake in putting sexuality within us. Indeed, our sexual nature is one of God's greatest gifts.

Every part of us interfaces with our sexual nature. Our bodies, our minds, and our spirits respond to sensuality on a number of levels. We feel the rush of attraction and the yearning to touch, to hold, and to express love physically. Our minds are sexually stimulated by what we see, what we read, and what we hear. Our spirits pine for union with another—for the God-designed ideal of two becoming one.

The way we interact with others shapes (and is shaped by) our sexual nature. In fact, "one of the most difficult assignments you'll ever have is to integrate your sexuality with the emotional, spiritual, social, and relational person you want to be."[1] The task is difficult because, like any extremely valuable and precious present, we have to keep and preserve the grand gift of sex.

You've been given strong and intense impulses. With just a spark, your yearning can ignite into a raging fire within you. Perhaps you've heard this idea from people who loosely quote 1 Corinthians 7:9: "It's better to marry than to burn with lust." (We have some friends who jokingly tell people they married just before bursting into flames.) Uncontrolled and untended sexual desire is lust—a fire that inflicts damage just as any unrestrained flame will.

At times, the sexual nature seems uncontrollable. Our natural sexual response ignites into lust, and the fire gets out of hand. Why does the fire burn out of control? Because *we stoke it.* No blaze can last without kindling. We feed the flames with the choices we make.

Natural sexual desires will not burn out of control by themselves. The fire of lust dies down without fuel. Now that's not to say those desires won't *feel* overwhelming at times. But if you refuse to stoke the fire, it will not overtake you. Only unrestrained urges rage uncontrollably. If you desire a clearly defined relationship—a clearly marked playing field—you must stop stoking the fire of sexual desire.

Believers face continual temptations to add fuel to the fire. The temptations come in many appealing forms: Four out of five sitcoms contain sexual content as do nine out of ten movies. In a recent study by The Kaiser Family Foundation, social scientists discovered that one-third of singles surveyed say the media encourages them to have sex.[2] Music videos titillate our senses and awaken our sexual desires. And next time you listen to the radio, try to discern the message in the music.

The temptation to stoke the fire comes through print as well. According to a recent study, "almost three-quarters of the articles published in women's magazines today are devoted to sexual topics."[3] And the Internet can take us directly and inconspicuously to the images that set us aflame.

As if the temptations from the media weren't enough, we're also bombarded by the sexual habits of our friends. What the proverbial "they" are doing or talking about influences your own tendency to stoke the fire.

None of these sources of temptation is itself inherently evil. Secular music is not the enemy, nor is television or cinema or the Internet. The question is this: Are you making choices to add fuel to a fire you want to control—or do you enjoy stoking the flames?

We've heard and read numerous accounts recently of young people engaging in oral sex. A college sophomore quoted in *Newsweek* said, "In high school, you could have oral sex and still call yourself a virgin. Now I'm like, 'Well, what makes one less intimate than the other?' "[4]

One is *not* less intimate than the other. Even secular psychologists quoted in *USA Weekend* (an August 2002 edition) admitted, "We need to move away from the idea that girls who engage in oral sex, but not intercourse, are 'technical' virgins—that you're not having sex because no one's penetrating you."[5]

The scary thing is that Christians are beginning to keep pace with the world in these sins, engaging in nonintercourse forms of intimacy and believing that removing the risk of pregnancy, as well as refraining from "going all the way," keeps a person a virgin for his or her wedding night. Christians have been fueling the fire of sexual lust, falling prey to the Enemy's attack on their minds, hearts, souls, and bodies.

Recent studies also show that one in ten Christians struggles with serious sexual addiction. One in ten! If this statistic doesn't shock you, consider your ten closest friends and imagine one of them struggling so fiercely with his sexual desires that he has begun to lose hope.

Sexual addiction can manifest itself in many ways. Locking the door to the computer room every night for a sexual escapade via the Internet can lead a believer to a place of bondage. So can continuing in a relationship that has become oversexualized and prematurely intimate.

We need to stop adding wood to the blaze! In order to rechalk the lines and affirm God's standards, we need to recognize what makes those lines blurred. Dr. Gregg Jantz wrote,

If we live in a culture that continually blares sexual messages, it's not enough to subconsciously turn down the volume. We'd better do some serious soul-searching to see how many of those messages we have unknowingly absorbed. Knowing what the messages are and how they are transmitted is one of the first steps to closing our hearts and ears to the unholy impulses they would stir within us.[6]

We are living in a world that inundates us with images of perverted sexuality. If we continue to expose ourselves to less than God's best, the fires of lust will never die down—and our relationships will face serious consequences.

GETTING BURNED

Our daughter Jocelyn recently discovered fire. We didn't think a nondescript book of matches lying around the house would entice a toddler, but she discovered it. She loves to look at the fire when one of us lights a match. She reaches for the flame, eyes wide with intrigue. She also adores the gas stove in our home. The blue, orange, and yellow flames captivate her.

Jocelyn has no idea what fire can do to her. She wants to play with it because it's attractive, desirable, different, and probably because we say no when she begins to reach for it. It's *forbidden,* so her longing increases.

Jocelyn doesn't know what the consequences of playing with fire might be. But as she grows, she will know what it's like to feel the heat of fire and even to be burned.

Proverbs 6:27-28 asks, "Can a man scoop fire into his lap without his clothes being burned? Can a man walk on hot coals without his feet being scorched?" Clearly, the answer is no. So why do we think that we can "scoop fire" into our laps by engaging in impurity—sexual and otherwise—while we're dating? Why do we assume we can "walk on the hot coals" of intimacy without being scorched?

The chapter continues: "So is he who sleeps with another man's wife; no one who touches her will go unpunished" (verse 29). You may think, *Well, I don't plan on sleeping with anyone—and especially not someone who is married.* But that narrows the principle that this Scripture teaches. The Lord uses an umbrella term in Scripture, *porneia,* to describe everything He considers sexually inappropriate. When you share *any* kind of premature intimacy with another, you betray the purity of another man's wife or another woman's husband.

We find that most Christians *know* or, at the very least, *sense* what is and is not sexually appropriate in a dating relationship. But we also see how often Christians jump into oversexualized relationships. As these Christians play with fire, they *are* being burned. The consequences of premature intimacy are very real.

Many Christians assume that they can avoid the "biggest" consequences if they simply hold back from sexual intercourse. If they don't go all the way, they think, they can't get pregnant or contract an STD. *Wrong!* Allow us to share with you some of the shocking realities of the STD epidemic. We bring these to light because Christians are catching these diseases—and not talking about it.

According to the Centers for Disease Control and Prevention, every STD that can be passed during intercourse can also be caught during oral sex. Heavy kissing can be enough to exchange the fluid necessary to contract some sexually transmitted diseases. Each day thirty-three thousand Americans become infected with an STD, and twenty-two thousand of these new STD infections are contracted by young people between the ages of fifteen and twenty-five. Today, one in every five Americans between the ages of fifteen and fifty-five is infected with at least one sexually transmitted disease. Do we think that these people are all non-Christians? That somehow because we're believers we can play with fire and not be burned?

The Centers for Disease Control and Prevention report that there are more than fifty known STDs. Some are incurable. Some can make you sterile. Over 40 percent of college students in the United States are infected with a venereal disease called human papillomavirus (HPV). HPV can cause cervical cancer and genital warts on both men and women that range in size from a small insect to the size of a cabbage.[7] We had never even heard of HPV before beginning the research for this chapter, yet 40 percent of college-aged people face a lifelong battle with a viral infection contracted during sexual activity (not just intercourse).

In our research we came across this heartbreaking account from an HPV-infected woman:

> There is no cure and no way out. At twenty-five, I have remained
> single and childless. That singleness is imposed upon me by my
> physical condition. The last four years of my life have been lived
> with chronic pain, two outpatient surgeries, multiple office bi-
> opsies, thousands of dollars in prescriptions, and no hope. The
> effect of this problem is one of severe, relentless infection. This
> condition can be so severe that the pain is almost unbearable, and
> a sexual relationship (or the possibility of marriage) is out of the
> question. The isolation is like a knife that cuts my heart out daily.
> Depression, rage, hopelessness, and a drastically affected social and
> religious life are the result.[8]

It's time for the church to wake up. Sexual activity before marriage has very real, life-altering consequences.

Pregnancy is also a very real threat to Christian couples who play with the fire of intimacy before marriage. In the last two years, two young women we knew—women raised in the church—became pregnant. They both chose to carry the babies to term and then gave the children up for adoption. These women had to deal with all the harsh realities of pregnancy—backaches, weight gain, swollen ankles, spider veins, stretch marks. And that's before labor and delivery!

Beyond those relatively minor physical challenges, they faced the heartbreaking surrender of the child they'd carried and nurtured for nine months. The wounds that their sexual promiscuity left on their body and their soul will take many years to heal.

We know that many of you will claim, "I'm not going to go all the way. It won't happen to me." But when you play with the fire of sexual impurity, you open yourself up to greater risk than you can calculate. If you keep in mind the serious consequences, you might be spurred to keep more clearly defined boundary lines.

By far the most widespread and devastating consequence of premarital sexual immorality is emotional devastation. Engaging in sexual activities before marriage leaves emotional scars that wound both now and later.

A recent study by the Institute for American Values evaluated the emotional state of single women who engaged in sexual activity without commitment. Forty percent of all college students reported having "hooked up." *Hooking up* was defined as having a one-time physical encounter that involved anything from kissing to intercourse, but with no expectations of a future relationship.

"Hook up" participants were asked to categorize their feelings a day or two after the event. They could select one or more words to describe their emotions. Sixty-four percent said "awkward" would best describe their feelings, while 57 percent chose "confused"; 44 percent selected "disappointed"; 27 percent "empty"; and 23 percent "exploited."[9]

These women immediately faced the emotional consequences of their inappropriate sexual activity. Outside a committed relationship, sexual experimentation left them feeling awkward, confused, disappointed, empty, and exploited—not emotions any of us would sign up to experience! And the stakes of emotional desolation after immoral sexual behavior only increase within a dating relationship.

Let us share two brief stories with you. These women are Christians who played with the fire of sexuality and got burned.

Danielle and her boyfriend began dating after meeting in a singles Bible study. Their physical relationship developed at what could be called a manageable pace. But the two kept pushing the limits further and seeing if they could maintain control.

Several months after starting to date this guy, Danielle e-mailed Jerusha, frantic for advice on how to step back physically. She wrote that she just wanted to have sex "sooooooooo badly" (and she used more *o*'s, but our space and your attention are limited) that she didn't know how to stop herself.

Then Danielle and Jerusha lost touch for a few months. Jerusha continued to pray and wonder and pray some more. Then she received another note from Danielle, saying that she'd made a terrible mistake and slept with Wayne—and that he had broken up with her a month and a half earlier.

Danielle found herself struggling with guilt, shame, and disillusionment. She could not believe she had shared herself so freely with someone who could cut things off so abruptly. She wrote that her heart couldn't seem to "get over it." She thought about the relationship all the time. She also felt distant from the Lord and felt unsure about how to regain intimacy with Him. Her emotions were a roller coaster of questions, anxieties, and heartbreak.

Danielle found that the consequences of sexual activity burn *now.* They sear the heart and spirit. They enslave the mind. When fulfilled, inappropriate sexual desires lead only to emotional regret.

Our dear friend Sammy also discovered that premature sexual experimentation burns *later.* Sammy dated the same guy for years. She thought maybe she'd marry him. It seemed as if it might work. They had grown up together at church, and everyone knew them "together."

But no one guessed that Sammy and her boyfriend kept secret an impure physical relationship. The touching—and beyond—had gotten out of control somewhere along the way, but after a while it had become such an established part of their relationship that though they never "planned" on falling again, nearly every time they got together, they did.

And then, as often happens to dating couples, they broke up. It took a long while for Sammy to process the hurt her sin had caused. She felt the scorching effects at the time, but what she didn't anticipate was how terribly the emotional wounds would impact her future marriage.

Sammy married an awesome Christian man, who forgave her and wanted to love her. Yet she couldn't find release or freedom from the memories of her sin, and she confessed to us that it affected their sexual relationship. Here she was supposed to enjoy the complete liberty of sexual expression that God intended for married couples, but the guilt and the emotional scars continued to plague her.

For instance, her husband didn't feel comfortable doing things that she and her ex-boyfriend had done. But a part of Sammy had been awakened and was now unsatisfied. Even more than that, Sammy couldn't *emotionally* disengage from what she had done before.

The emotional consequences of sexual promiscuity go far beyond the present. They impact the heart later as well. Singer Kim Hill puts it well:

The decision to have sex outside of marriage results in a slow, subtle kind of death. It's the death of innocence and purity. The shattering of dreams. The numbing of a once vibrant, youthful spirit. The word abstinence implies denial and all sorts of negative restrictions. In truth, though, abstinence means wholeness and freedom and peace. A life of virtue can be a difficult road, but it's a road of promise and excellence, and one without regret.[10]

"A road of promise and excellence and one without regret." When compared to the possibility of facing any of the consequences we've discussed here in brutal detail, that's a road worth taking.

The Fireplace

When we lived in Colorado, the temperature dropped well below freezing on some nights. Bundling up inside the house with warm blankets, a mug of steaming hot coffee, and a fire could not have been more perfect. But we never made the fire in the middle of our living room. Why would we when there was a *place* for the fire? Containing the blaze allowed us to enjoy the beauty without the danger.

We've talked about sexuality and sexual desire as a fire. Now it's time to look at where God intended that fire be kept. The Lord designed marriage as the fireplace. Focus on the Family's book about sex, *No Apologies,* shares this:

Sex is risky, but marriage…makes the risk worth taking. It's the bond that preserves and protects. It's the place where interpersonal understanding has a chance to flower, where emotional bonds can grow deep and strong over time…Marriage is the only thing strong enough to contain the power of sex and make it positive and constructive.[11]

These aren't merely nice ideas. These are paraphrases of God's truths—and never is this truth more powerful than in 1 Corinthians 7. Read how the modern translation *The Message* presents God's intention for marriage and sex:

> Now, getting down to the questions you asked…. First, Is it a good thing to have sexual relations? Certainly—but only within a certain context. It's good for a man to have a wife, and for a woman to have a husband. Sexual drives are strong, but marriage is strong enough to contain them and provide for a balanced and fulfilling sexual life in a world of sexual disorder. (verses 1-2)

Many Christian couples build fires outside of marriage and then try to do damage control to limit the extent of the devastation. Instead of waiting for God's provision of the fireplace, they run ahead with activities they think they can keep safe or under control. But God wants us to have a bigger vision for our sexuality. He wants us to have a grander view of marriage, that we might *want* the fire of our sexuality to burn and be built only there.

The great preacher Elton Trueblood once eloquently defined marriage from his pulpit as two persons being so "caught up by a dream and a purpose bigger than themselves that they work through the years, in spite of repeated disappointment, to make the dream come true."[12] Marriage is a dream and a purpose bigger than an individual. It was instituted by God as part of His "very good" creation. And sex is *such* a good thing—such a sacred, holy, perfectly designed and powerful thing—that it *has* to be kept for the proper time and place. Otherwise its goodness is lost or spoiled or destroyed.

We love the way Proverbs 5:18-19 reads in *The Living Bible:* "Let your manhood be a blessing; rejoice in the wife of your youth. Let her charms and tender embrace satisfy you. Let her love alone fill you with delight." The *New Living Translation* ends that passage with "May you always be captivated by her love."

The scope of this chapter in a book on defining relationships well simply cannot contain all that God has to say when it comes to sexuality and marriage. We suggest that before you DTR with anyone, you develop a vision for God's great purpose in creating us as sexual beings.[13] If you take time to know what God has to say, we're confident you'll desire to keep the fire in its proper place.

RECHALKING THE LINES

We've seen that God created us as sexual beings, that we can add wood (or *not* add wood) to the fire of sexual desire, and that letting the fire burn outside of its proper place can have very serious consequences. Now it's time to go back to God's playing field and discover how you and the person you're dating can rechalk the lines so that your relationship might mature within the framework He's designed for sexuality.

First, here are two quick things to use as a springboard for a personal DTR before you talk with the person you're dating.

1. Put Sex in the Context of Your Whole Life

You may find it helpful to write down all the things that are important to you in life. Then consider where and how sex fits into that picture. You will probably see that sex is not as all-encompassing as it sometimes seems to be. When you can logically think through your priorities and how sex outside the context of marriage could impact them, you'll be better equipped to make decisions based on *life,* not any single moment in time. If you find yourself ranking sex above family, friendships, goals, dreams, and even God, you will want to reconsider the emphasis you've placed on this one aspect of your being.

2. Recognize the Time Delay

As a believer, you will find two messages competing for your attention. The first comes from the Lord, who commands that sexual expression be saved for marriage. That means *wait.* The second message blaring in your ears is that sexual fulfillment is something worth having *now.*

These contradictory messages become more challenging to reconcile when the possibility of marriage is in the distant future: after college, after you get your master's degree, after you get your career off the ground, and so on. The push to get a college education, to establish a career, and to stay on top of financial challenges has moved marriage into the "out of the question for now" category for many singles. Although hormones rage the most fiercely between ages sixteen and twenty-six, permanent, committed love within marriage is simply not a viable option for many people in this age range. In fact, the average male today doesn't seriously consider marriage until age twenty-six. You can see that a significant time delay exists between the time hormones develop and the time when sexual desires might be fulfilled in the God-ordained way.

If you can see sex within the context of your whole life, you will be able to not only acknowledge but also reconcile this time delay factor. Knowing that you're in a holding pattern because of the greater design for your life will enable you to make stronger commitments for a longer haul.[14]

Now, here are six things you can discuss within a DTR to help you maintain the personal commitments you've made to the Lord about your sexuality. These six points will also encourage the person you're dating.

1. Agree Upon a Specific Physical Limit for Your Relationship

This statement may seem obvious, but it's important to remember that you need to deal in specifics, not general categories. This discussion requires some maturity on your part. Perhaps talking about different levels of kissing embarrasses you. Get over it. Without a specific boundary, you'll find yourself questioning and wondering.

Some friends of ours recently told us that the way they defined their physical relationship began by the guy trying to hold her hand. He figured that if she held back, that was DTR enough. Not so for the woman he was dating. She was confused by his actions and wanted to know their intentions as a couple. They eventually recognized the need to specifically verbalize what their boundaries would be.

2. Affirm Together That You Must Trust God, Not Yourselves

Dwight L. Moody once preached, "Trust in yourself and you are doomed to disappointment; trust in God, and you are never to be confounded in time or eternity." You cannot remain physically pure as a couple in your own strength. Most of you *know* this, but it's not enough to have this head knowledge. In a successful DTR you both will confirm *out loud* that the two of you place your trust in God. This vocal acknowledgment, said prayerfully, will help move your understanding from head to heart and then to action.

Psalm 16:8 can serve as a reminder verse for the two of you: "I know the LORD is always with me. I will not be shaken, for he is right beside me" (NLT).

3. Devise a Plan for Success

Don't mistake merely knowing about the consequences for having an actual plan. All the information and knowledge in the world won't do a couple an ounce of good unless they use it as raw material for something even more important: choices, decisions, and action.

Both of you may have grown up in a church that reinforced the consequences of premarital sexual experimentation. You may read and reread the section on consequences in this book. But until you plan what you will do to avoid these consequences, you're little better off than someone who isn't equipped with this information.

Planning together for success means agreeing on places you will and won't go alone as well as what you will and won't do on your dates. Planning means purposefully determining which activities will encourage you in your commitments and which ones will not.

Another aspect of planning is reevaluation. When something doesn't work, have a DTR to reestablish your boundaries. Don't let things slide when you've stepped over the lines.

A reminder verse for this aspect of a well-defined physical relationship is found in Proverbs 14: "Do not those who plot evil go astray? But those who plan what is good find love and faithfulness" (verse 22).

4. Verify As a Couple That the Boundaries Have Fallen in Pleasant Places

This image comes directly from Scripture. In Psalm 16:5-6 David thanks the Lord first for His provision: "LORD, you have assigned me my portion and my cup; you have made my lot secure." He continues by confirming that "the boundary lines have fallen for me in pleasant places." The Lord blesses you with the amazing freedom of being able to date. That freedom comes within certain boundaries—*pleasant* boundaries.

You may smirk at the notion, but consider being set down in the Australian outback with no water, no compass, and no crocodile hunter to guide you out. You would probably feel frightened rather than free or adventurous at this point. We need—even crave—boundaries because they make things safe and, yes, pleasant.

If, as a couple, you can acknowledge that the boundaries you've agreed upon together are "good" and "pleasant," you'll be much more likely to respect and keep them than if you view them simply as rules. Bring back to mind Psalm 16:5-6 when you feel that what is really good and pleasant lies on the other side of the boundary. You haven't been betrayed by the Lord. Choose to see that the boundary lines God has set for you have fallen in pleasant places.

5. Tie a String Around Your Finger

Well, maybe not *literally*, but during a DTR we suggest that you select and later use a visual reminder of your commitment to purity. It can be any object that reminds you of your core values. Both of you can agree to keep the object close to you and visible throughout a date.

Many young women wear a "purity ring," given to them by someone who cares about their chastity and wants to encourage them in it. If you haven't already been given such a gift, consider purchasing something for yourself. Choose as this "purity present" an item that speaks of the beauty and splendor of purity.

If that idea turns the stomachs of some of you guys out there, think of an item that speaks to you of masculinity. After all, a true man waits for marriage. The item a guy might choose to represent his commitment to chastity can be something that suggests unyielding strength and dignity.

If you can't afford to buy an item, write a vow of purity *for* yourself and maybe even *to* your desired future spouse. Type the pledge and place it in your purse, in your wallet, on your dashboard—wherever it can be not only handy but visible. (Hey, you could even laminate it. Wouldn't that be snazzy?)

A *visual* reminder does you no good tucked away in the sock drawer! Think of it this way: Your parents—or, worse, your grandparents!—walk in on you making out with someone. Just seeing them is enough to stop your desire cold. Seeing a girl's purity ring, or catching a glimpse of a pledge taped inside someone's car can have the same impact but with a positive spin: You want to stop because of your commitment to God, not because you're caught.

6. Decide Now to Periodically Reevaluate

It's essential that together you determine a boundary line that both of you can respect and maintain. If you don't agree to refresh that commitment continually, however, you may find yourselves either forgetful or facing increasing desire.

There used to be an ad campaign for potato chips with the slogan "Bet you can't eat just one." When it comes to physical contact, couples often reach a point where just "one" isn't enough. Holding hands or a quick good-night kiss just doesn't stave off the increasing hunger for affectionate touching.

At this point you may want to have a DTR to interrupt the natural flow of physical contact in your relationship. If you don't, you'll find yourself ravenous and your relationship more and more sexualized.

Any regular sexual contact you've established can become an inevitable part of your relationship. You may find that you two are making out when you had assured yourself you'd just watch a DVD together. Or you may notice that your dates *always* end in touching. Or you realize that physical affection has become the unavoidable conclusion of every interaction.

If you find yourself in this kind of situation, consider fasting from any and all touching. Good friends of ours who were just recently married discovered in the course of their dating and engagement that their hunger for physicality built up quickly. They determined to fast now and then; they would take a break from physically expressing their affection for each other. These times of fasting helped them refocus on what mattered most in their relationship: communication, respect, trust, all the good stuff that made them want to date and marry each other. What they learned was that not only could their physical drives be controlled, but the hunger they felt didn't have to be satisfied.

This couple succeeded in part because they were willing to continually reassess their physical relationship. Had they simply "gone with the flow" their relationship could have been seriously burned.

WRAPPING THINGS UP

We want to reiterate how helpful it can be to pursue outside help and support for your relationship. Each of you should seek out someone to hold you accountable to your physical boundaries, someone older and more mature in the faith who is able to speak into your life effectively. You do need to talk about the fire of your sex drive—just not necessarily with your date! Find someone who can hold you accountable for the thoughts and feelings that may sometimes try to overtake you. In his book *There's a Lot More to Health Than Not Being Sick,* Bruce Larson points out,

> Behavioral sciences in recent years have expounded the simple
> truth that "behavior that is observed changes." *People who are*
> *accountable* by their own choice to a group of friends…to a pas-
> toral counselor, to a study or prayer group, *are people serious*
> *about changing their behavior,* and they are finding that change

is possible.... If only God knows what I'm doing, since I know He won't tell, I tend to make all kinds of excuses for myself. But if I must report to another or a group of others, I begin to monitor my behavior. If someone is keeping an eye on me, my behavior improves.[15]

Finally, we'd like to close on this note. John R. Rice once said, "No matter what a man's past may have been, his future is spotless." If you've gone too far sexually in the past, you can experience God's complete forgiveness. All you have to do is confess your sin to the Lord and ask for His cleansing. Reread and be encouraged by this familiar verse from 1 John 1:9, translated with fresh power by J. B. Phillips: "If we freely admit that we have sinned, we find God utterly reliable and straightforward—he forgives our sins and makes us thoroughly clean from all that is evil."

Not only can you start now with a clean slate, a spotless future, but you are not doomed to repeat the mistakes that you have made. Once you've been forgiven, you need to move forward with a new commitment to holiness and to setting yourself apart from sin. This life of purity is what God desires for each of his beloved ones.

Keep Paul's words from Philippians 3:13-14 in mind: "But one thing I do: Forgetting what is behind and straining toward what is ahead, I press on toward the goal to win the prize for which God has called me heavenward in Christ Jesus."

How Character Defines Relationships

One overarching theme we pray you've sensed as you've read the previous chapters is that godly, healthy relationships are built and maintained by godly, healthy people. People of character. People defined by their virtues. You simply cannot expect to define a relationship well unless *you've* been defined by the characteristics that encourage godly interaction with the opposite sex.

The closer a man and woman draw to the Lord, the better able they are to relate to each other. Growing close to God enables Him to build His character in them. Furthermore, as men and women become characterized by the holy, pure, and admirable attributes of righteousness, they will be able to define their relationships in a more godly way.

So, to conclude this book, we would like to look at how men and women can better define their character. We believe that this devotional will equip you to better protect yourself, know yourself, and direct the course of your relationships according to God's principles.

We need to turn to the ultimate source—God's Word—to discover what character qualities should define a person who can then define his relationships well. So, this chapter will be like a mini-Bible study more than anything else. In fact, we want you to use it as a five-day or ten-day devotional.

We've selected five men and five women from Scripture, individuals whose character defined their relationships with others. Each of these role models provides us with a glimpse into the very heart of godly masculine and feminine character.

As you probably already know, men and women approach the opposite sex with distinctive thoughts, desires, and expectations. It's helpful to learn about the different ways God has created us and called us to express His character. That's why we have divided the study below into two sections, based on gender. We suggest that you first look at the devotional based on your gender.

It's important, though, that men and women understand each other as well as themselves. So we also encourage you to read and process the devotionals for the other sex. Some of the questions may not be pertinent to you, but considering the issues and themes will be invaluable in helping you both choose a partner of godly character and appreciate the opposite sex as a whole.

We believe that you will also notice a great deal of crossover in the traits we've chosen for men and women. Many are virtues that *both* sexes would benefit from developing. As you read through the biblical stories and the questions for consideration, ask the Holy Spirit to illuminate how you might be changed by His truth.

Finally, depending on the maturity and depth of your relationship, you may even consider using this book as a couple's devotional. You could include other couples and create a small-group Bible study. Just remember, if you use this tool in such a way, you may start forging strong emotional and spiritual bonds. Be sure your relationship is ready for such a step before you proceed.

DAY 1 (MEN): ZACCHAEUS—DEFINED BY REPENTANCE

Scriptures: Luke 19:1-10; 2 Corinthians 5:17

Luke 19 opens with the story of a little man (literally, a short guy) whose relationships with others were transformed because his character became defined by repentance—a change of the mind and will. We're talking about Zacchaeus.

Zacchaeus came on the biblical scene late in Jesus' ministry. In fact, soon after his meeting with Zacchaeus, Jesus entered Jerusalem in triumph, only to be crucified the following week.

As Luke 19 begins, we find Jesus entering the city of Jericho—the ancient city whose walls had come crashing down after the obedient and courageous Joshua led the Israelites in a mighty display of God's power and sovereignty.

Jericho had history, and so did one of its most infamous residents, the tax collector Zacchaeus. Working for the Roman IRS, Zacchaeus only had to submit to Caesar a certain required amount of money. Whatever else the tax gatherer could squeeze out of the people would line his pockets and pack his pantry.

The region surrounding Jericho prospered, and Zacchaeus grew rich through exploitation and manipulation. Scripture tells us that he was the "chief tax collector" (verse 2), which indicates he oversaw the entire district and had any number of despicable money-mongers like himself working beneath him.

Zacchaeus hardly fit the profile for the most likely candidate to earnestly pursue God, yet we're told that when he heard Jesus approach, Zacchaeus eagerly entered the throng of people gathered to check out Jesus.

Luke reveals that Zacchaeus "wanted to see who Jesus was, but being a short man he could not, because of the crowd" (verse 3). This didn't daunt the pesky little tax collector. He climbed a sycamore, a sprawling tree that could grow up to forty feet high. The short trunk and sturdy branches made it a perfect fit for Zacchaeus.

Meanwhile, Jesus came closer, so close, in fact, that He stood just below the tree. Jesus looked up and called to Zacchaeus, "Come down immediately. I must stay at your house today." In an instant, Zacchaeus changed. He came down at once to welcome Jesus ("gladly," Luke tells us in verse 6) not merely into his home but into his heart.

You can almost hear the crowd (who may have pushed Zacchaeus into his sycamore perch) gasp and mutter among themselves, "What in the world is Jesus doing? This guy is the worst of all sinners. He's treated us terribly all these years." Before meeting Jesus, Zacchaeus was known for his selfishness, greed, manipulation, and control, and those traits defined his relationships with others. But in verse 8, Luke unveils a miraculous transformation in his character. Zacchaeus announced, "Look, Lord! Here and now I give half of my possessions to the poor, and if I have cheated anybody out of anything, I will pay back four times the amount."

No doubt with a beaming smile on His face, Jesus responded, "Today salvation has come to this house" (verse 9). The redeemed Zacchaeus had been forever changed. Christ with him altered the way he interacted with others. No longer marked by deceit and exploitation, Zacchaeus's relationships became defined by God's desire, mercy, and righteousness.

Zacchaeus had lived a less-than-perfect life. Like each one of us. We've all sinned against the Lord and others, treating brothers and sisters with selfishness and duplicity. But Zacchaeus's life teaches us that when we meet Jesus and repent, we become new. C. S. Lewis wrote,

> A live body is not one that never gets hurt, but one that can to
> some extent repair itself. In the same way a Christian is not a man

who never goes wrong, but a man who is enabled to repent and pick himself up and begin over again after each stumble—because the Christ-life is inside him, repairing him all the time.[1]

With repentance, you are transformed. Christ repairs you. And then He repairs your relationships. No matter what your relationships have been like in the past, as a man in Christ you can choose to repent and live a new life. Zacchaeus had one of the worst starts to fellowship with others that we can imagine. But his past did not determine his future. God did. Yesterday's mistakes do not govern your today.

As a man of God, you can be transformed like Zacchaeus was and change today, as he did, the way you relate. Become a man defined by repentance and watch God transform your relationships.

Questions for Consideration

1. What does 2 Corinthians 5:17 say happens to those in Christ?
2. In Zacchaeus's life, the old went and the new came, just as 2 Corinthians 5:17 promises. In what ways are you different because you have encountered Jesus?
3. Think about your past relationships with both men and women. In what ways have you interacted that would be considered old or untransformed?
4. Are you ready to make the commitment to repentance—to authentic change—and the new life? Why or why not?
5. What specific changes in your relationships with others might come as a result of your repentance and new life?

DAY 2 (MEN): JONATHAN—DEFINED BY AUTHENTIC MALE FRIENDSHIP

Scriptures: 1 Samuel 18–20; Proverbs 27:17

On first glance, 1 Samuel 18–20 may seem like an odd place to turn for a study on how friendship between men builds character. The chapters are in fact riddled with the murderous attempts of King Saul on David's life.

Saul hated David with a consuming passion. David had defeated the Philistine giant Goliath to end an impasse with Israel's enemy, and he had proven himself useful to the king as a musician with healing skill, yet Saul despised David with such fervor that he plotted on six different occasions to kill his servant.

Into the chaos and madness of this story, God weaves the story of an authentic friendship. Intertwined with the recounting of David's life is the tale of another man, Jonathan. After David slew Goliath, Scripture tells us that he met Jonathan, the king's son. An immediate bond of love grew between them, and Jonathan made a special vow—a covenant—to be David's friend.

Jonathan risked much to uphold his promise of friendship. On more than one occasion, he warned David of his father's plans to assassinate him. He also spoke to Saul on David's behalf, urging the king to recall the good that David had done for the nation and for him.

Eventually, however, Jonathan realized that his father would stop at nothing to murder David. Saul commanded Jonathan to assist him in a treacherous plot by bringing David to him. Jonathan not only refused, but he also helped David escape.

Against the 1 Samuel 18–20 backdrop of threat and tragedy, we see Jonathan and David talking together and praying to God as friends. They continually kept each other accountable to their vows and thus challenged each other to be men of greater integrity and courage. Eugene Peterson wrote that this story teaches "friendship *forms*." He explains:

Friendship is a much underestimated aspect of spirituality. It's every bit as significant as prayer and fasting.... It's a great thing to be a Jonathan. Without Jonathan, David was at risk of either abandoning his vocation...or developing a murderous spirit of retaliation."[2]

God used Jonathan's friendship to help form David into the man after His own heart that this young warrior would become.

As the son of the king of Israel, Jonathan must have been accustomed to getting what he wanted from whomever he wanted. He could have defined himself by using people and things to get the most out of life. But he chose the path of authentic friendship, and because of this godly virtue, the relationships Jonathan had with others grew in strength and health. Pastor and teacher Jack Hayford articulates,

Contrary to popular belief, men aren't born. Children are born—men are *formed*. And the Bible says men help form each other. Carved, designed and shaped—males are processed into true manhood. At the core of that process is one crucial component: man-to-man relationship. Prioritizing the cultivation of such relationships according to God's created order is in line with His blueprint for full manhood. One of the chief scalpels that God has chosen for shaping us into His image is the dynamic of personal friendships—man-to-man relationships. This is an essential, practical biblical principle, and one of a man's key starting places.[3]

Before they can define relationships with the opposite sex well, men need to be defined by genuine male companionship—the kind that forms, molds, and shapes both of the individuals involved into what God desires, not merely the guys-night-out kind of friendship that the world seems to encourage.

When men come together in true friendship as Jonathan and David did, their characters are sharpened, their vision of who God would have them be is refreshed, and their commitment to uphold righteousness is renewed.

Questions for Consideration

1. According to Proverbs 27:17, what happens when men interact?
2. List the relationships you have with other men. In what ways does each of these men sharpen (or not sharpen!) you? Be specific.
3. In what ways is God using you to sharpen these men as you interact with them?
4. What can you do to encourage growth in the relationships you have with other men?
5. What have you learned (or could you learn) from your male friendships that will improve your interaction with the opposite sex?

DAY 3 (MEN): DANIEL—DEFINED BY CONSISTENT FAITH

Scriptures: Daniel 1:8-21; 4:33-37; 5:17-31; 6:4,10,26-27; Isaiah 26:3

Steadfast, steady, even. Reliable, unswerving, unfailing. These words capture the essence of *consistency,* and few biblical characters exemplify this characteristic better than Daniel.

Daniel began life with the odds stacked against him. King Nebuchadnezzar of Babylon besieged the city of Jerusalem and carried off the articles of the temple as well as some noble and royal Israelite men to serve him.

An apt, quick, and qualified young man, Daniel matched the king's standards for a palace steward. So the Babylonians carted him off to be trained for three years in language, literature, and civic duty. At the end of that time, Daniel would enter the royal service.

When Daniel arrived at the palace, he found that each day he and the other Israelites would receive food and wine from the king's table. Maybe things weren't going to be so bad in exile. No doubt the finest meat and drink that Babylon had to offer would be available to Daniel.

But the food of Nebuchadnezzar's table was offered to idols before it went to the king and his servants. The Babylonian cooks prepared ceremonially unclean animals in ways that broke the regulations of Mosaic law. Basically, the food was contaminated.

At this point, young Daniel made a decision that would define his character and his relationships with others for the rest of his life. He "resolved not to defile himself with the royal food and wine" (Daniel 1:8). Not only did this choice affect his relationship with God, but it affected his relationship with the palace officials and with the king himself. Daniel's actions showed his godly character and witnessed to all those surrounding him.

Throughout the book of Daniel, we trace how this early commitment played out in a life consistently lived for the glory of God. Three other times Daniel faced tests of his dedication "not to defile himself." And each time God received glory and changed the lives of those with whom Daniel interacted.

The first occasion arose when the king called upon Daniel to interpret a disturbing dream. (For a fascinating read, check out the details in Daniel 4.) The dream foretold a bad end for Nebuchadnezzar, and Daniel could have shirked his responsibility to God and glossed over the foreboding details. But Daniel remained consistent in his integrity and righteousness. The result? In the end, Nebuchadnezzar praised God and honored and glorified Him. Daniel's steady life in God influenced his relationship with

Nebuchadnezzar and, by God's grace, resulted in the dramatic furthering of God's kingdom.

In the second instance, Nebuchadnezzar's grandson summoned Daniel to decipher a puzzling inscription on the castle wall. The new ruler promised huge rewards if he could interpret the words (see Daniel 5:16-17). Again, Daniel had to choose whether to reveal that this message spelled trouble for the king. In unswerving determination, Daniel forsook the offerings of the king and spoke honestly with Belshazzar. God rewarded Daniel's consistency by granting him the king's favor despite the interpretation. Daniel reaped the benefit of a relationship built on unchanging devotion to God's standards.

The greatest challenge came last when King Darius issued a decree that prohibited prayer. By this time, Daniel was an old man. Having lived a life of consistency with which, as Scripture tells us, no man could find fault (see Daniel 6:4), Daniel continued in open prayer "just as he had done before" (Daniel 6:10).

You may be able to guess what happened next (it's one of Sunday school's most thrilling tales!). Daniel was thrown into the lion's den, God miraculously rescued him, and the king not only reversed the decree but issued an edict that all people praise and worship Daniel's God as the living God. Daniel 6 closes with the report that Daniel prospered thereafter.

Once again, Daniel's consistent walk with the Lord led others to worship God and brought blessings on Daniel's relationships with others. As Daniel interacted with people, he remained steadfast in his commitments to God. Not only was Daniel's life blessed, but God used his example to draw others to Him.

As Oswald Chambers wrote, "A life of faith is not a life of one glorious mountaintop experience after another, like soaring on eagles' wings, but is a life of day-in and day-out consistency; a life of walking without fainting."[4] When you walk without fainting in consistent devotion to the

Lord, you will have an impact on others. As you relate to them, they will see a difference in you and be drawn to God. What a privilege and what a responsibility! As you choose to be defined by consistent devotion to the Lord, you will reap a rich harvest in your own life as well as in your relationships with others.

Questions for Consideration

1. In what ways has inconsistency in your own life negatively affected your relationships with others? Be specific.
2. Daniel chose not to defile himself with food from the king's table. He forewent pleasure in order to serve God with steadfastness. What pleasures that may come with relationships are you willing to surrender in order to live a life consistent with God's standards?
3. According to Isaiah 26:3, what promise does the Lord make to those who walk steadfastly or consistently?
4. Why might "perfect peace" affect your ability to relate to the opposite sex?
5. What specific character quality would you like to have consistently mark your relationships with women?

Day 4 (Men): John the Baptist—Defined by Humility

Scriptures: Luke 1:13-15; Matthew 11:11; John 3:22-30; Proverbs 15:33; 18:12

As an ancient adage says, "Self praise smells bad." In other words, pride stinks. The sick stench of self-absorbed people pollutes our world. Prideful people steamroll over others. They seek their own gain, sometimes not knowing, sometimes not caring what the cost may be to their relationships.

Humility, on the other hand, refreshes the senses with love, grace, and mercy. People of modest disposition and deference to others bless all who come into contact with them. Those defined by humility build relationships characterized by honor, respect, and reverence.

Throughout Scripture, God commands us believers to show humility toward others (see 1 Peter 5:5), to humbly consider others as better than ourselves (see Philippians 2:3), and to humble ourselves before Him (see James 4:10). Jesus Himself displayed such humility and modeled for all men how to relate to others.

But let's be honest: Humility is no easy virtue to understand and live out. Men in particular seem prone to struggle with pride as they relate to others. We recently spoke frankly with a close friend about his past interactions with women, and he confessed that the demise of each of his relationships could be traced to his own pride and selfishness—to a lack of humility.

You may be thinking, *Jesus is God; of course He could act in humility.* Lest we think that humility requires too much of a mere man, the Lord provides us with a living example of authentic humility in John the Baptist. By anyone's standards, John had every right to think highly of himself. An angel foretold his conception and revealed that "many will rejoice because of his birth, for he will be great in the sight of the Lord" (Luke 1:14-15).

John was set apart to live as a Nazirite (having vowed to abstain from alcohol and never cut his hair as a sign of devotion to God). He lived in the desert, wore clothes of animal hair, and subsisted on a diet of locusts and wild honey. According to God's plan, John matured into a prophet and teacher. People flocked to hear his message, though he seemed to do nothing to attract them.

Jesus declared that "among those born of women there has not risen anyone greater than John the Baptist" (Matthew 11:11). If Jesus had said this about most men, their head might do a bit of swelling and their manner of interacting with people might change ever so slightly. Or, more likely, ever so *greatly.* But John the Baptist refused to define himself pridefully. In John 3, we see his genuine humility.

Many people had come to receive John's baptism, while Jesus himself also baptized across the river Jordan. Some of John's followers got a little peeved and commented on Jesus' success on the other side of the river. Instead of puffing himself up and quoting the words Jesus spoke about him, John responded in humility, "He must become greater; I must become less" (John 3:30). John didn't try to impress the people around him; he didn't try to manipulate their affections or keep them for himself. John recognized his place before Jesus, the incarnate God, and so he placed himself in proper relationship with others.

Jerry Bridges wrote about how humility before God affects our relationships with people:

> Humility before God is basic to all our relationships in life. We
> cannot begin to experience humility in any other relationship until
> we experience a deep and profound humility in our attitude toward
> God. When we are conscious of our (sinful) creature relationship
> to an infinitely majestic and holy God, we will not wish to selfishly
> [interact] with others.[5]

John's willingness to decrease meant Christ's increase, and it also strengthened his human relationships. Able to diminish himself in order to elevate others, John could relate to people humbly and as a servant, just as Christ commanded. So, as you deal with others, let humility mark your attitude and actions. Let an active surrender to decrease define your character, and you will see the results reflected in your relationships with others.

Proverbs 15:33 and 18:12 clearly state that "humility comes before honor." If you desire the honor of strong relationships, humility must come first.

Questions for Consideration

1. Based on John's story, define *humility.*
2. What impact did humility have on the way John related to others? Be specific.
3. Proverbs 18:12 has often been paraphrased as "pride goes before a fall." In what ways have you seen pride go before a fall in your relationships with the opposite sex?
4. What tangible steps might you take to exercise humility as you interact with women?
5. In what ways might God honor your relationships and your life as you live humbly before Him and others?

Day 5 (Men): Jesus—Defined by Servant Leadership

Scriptures: John 13:1-17; Matthew 20:26-28; Ephesians 5:23

A curious paradox runs throughout Scripture, a turning-on-the-head of everything that seems sensible. Matthew 20:26-27—"Whoever wants to become great among you must be your servant, and whoever wants to be first must be your slave"—strikes us as not only illogical but uncomfortable.

What man does not crave greatness? In the deepest part of our nature, we men want to have an impact on the world and on others. We yearn to direct and to guide, to shape and to influence. In essence, we men want to lead.

But to lead by serving? by making oneself a slave? How could that make sense?

The truth is that great men lead by serving: "The Son of Man did not come to be served, but to serve, and to give his life as a ransom for many" (Matthew 20:28). Christ is looking for men of greatness, men who will lead and influence. But He asks those men to serve first, to give themselves up for others. No character quality is more essential to relationships than that which Christ Himself modeled perfectly in His relationships—servant leadership.

In John 13 we witness one of the most intimate moments of fellowship between Christ and His people. In the account of the Upper Room feast, we see Jesus interacting with the twelve men He had handpicked to shape the future of His church. And what method does Christ choose to instruct his disciples in leadership? A lecture on the need for vision or for determination? A PowerPoint presentation on the top ten qualities of a good leader?

No, He washed their feet. Their dirty, wearing-sandals-and-walking-through-the-dusty-streets-of-Jerusalem feet. Without pomp or circumstance, the Lord removed His outer garment and picked up a towel. He poured water into a bowl and knelt at the feet of each of the twelve whom He loved. He tenderly and purposefully cleansed their feet just as the lowliest servant would normally do.

What an incredible action to witness! The Creator of the universe chose to define His relationships with His disciples by serving them! And then He asked the Twelve to lead others by doing the same in His name: "Now that I, your Lord and Teacher, have washed your feet, you also should wash one another's feet. I have set you an example that you should do as I have done for you" (John 13:14-15).

Scripture reports that this act "showed [the disciples] the full extent of his love" (John 13:1). The greatest expression of love you can show others is to genuinely serve them, as Christ modeled. A servant leader gains the respect and admiration of others. A servant leader develops and then enjoys strong relationships grounded in love and self-sacrifice.

God calls you to live as a man defined by servant leadership, and He may eventually call you to servant-lead a woman in marriage. Ephesians 5:23 teaches that "the husband is the head of the wife as Christ is the head of the church." This verse ranks as one of the most misunderstood and misused scriptures in the entire Bible. If you look at Ephesians 5:23 through the window of the Upper Room where Christ washed His disciples' feet, there's no doubt that what Christ calls husbands to do is give themselves to their wives in loving service as He gave Himself to His disciples.

Servant leadership marks a great man. Servant leadership defines a godly husband. You can choose now, as a single, to define yourself as a servant leader, preparing yourself for a future of promise, a future of healthy, godly relationships with others.

Questions for Consideration

1. What is the world's definition of leadership and greatness?

2. Who do you think has greater impact—a worldly leader or a servant leader? Why?

3. In what ways might exercising worldly leadership affect your relationships with others? How might servant leadership, exemplified by Christ, affect your interaction with others?

4. Judas was still in the room when Christ served His disciples. Jesus washed Judas's feet even though He knew Judas would betray Him. Sometimes God calls us to servant-lead even our enemies. Imagine that you've recently broken up with a woman who's made herself your enemy, betraying your trust and wounding you deeply. What specifically does Christ's example encourage you to do in such a situation?

5. How might defining yourself as a servant leader in your present relationships prepare you for the future?

DAY 1 (WOMEN): ESTHER—DEFINED BY CONFIDENCE

Scriptures: Esther 4:14-16, 5:2; Psalm 71:5; Hebrews 13:5-6,8

Esther's story sounds like a fairy tale. Born an orphan and raised by cousins, Esther didn't start life with the greatest pedigree or potential. A parentless Jewish girl stuck in a foreign, pagan land as a result of her people's exile didn't count for much in the world's eyes.

But in God's plan the failed marriage of the king of Persia coincided with Esther's development as a young woman. In his hunt for a virgin queen, King Xerxes brought this orphan teen into his palace where she received a year of royal beauty treatments, training in grace and charm, and every princesslike attention that girls dream of. All of this was to prepare her to meet Xerxes and possibly win his approval. All of it was apparently done to please one man—the king. But we'll soon see that God had far more exalted purposes.

During his search for "love," King Xerxes discovered Esther and favored her above all. His quest for a queen ended, and Esther ascended to the throne. This, however, did not complete God's plan; it merely set the stage. Unaware of Esther's background, King Xerxes was hoodwinked by a conniving, villainous palace official into a plot to destroy Esther's people. Mordecai, the cousin who raised Esther, told Esther about the conspiracy against the Jews. Esther had to decide whether she would act to save the Jews from annihilation.

Let's take a break from the action of the story for a moment and look at Esther's journey to the throne from another angle. What do you think Esther thought of herself? It's safe to say that most women born into the world without the love and security that parents give, and into a foreign place where most viewed her and her religious beliefs with contempt, would be thought of as a nothing. Most women would *feel* like nothing too.

It's also safe to postulate that after a year of the best facials, manicures, pedicures, and makeup artistry, this girl would not only look like a queen but be treated like one. Esther could easily have defined herself by what others thought and moved from deep self-doubt to overconfidence—until her people's lives were threatened, that is.

Then she couldn't rely on beauty and poise. What if the king chose to include her in the massacre? Should she hide her true self? If she did, could she live with the knowledge that she had allowed the slaughter of so many innocent relations?

Yet to go to the king and plead for her people was not only risky, but strictly forbidden. No matter how confident she might be that her *appearance* pleased the king, she could not guarantee that he would listen to her heart. Esther could have been thrown back to the insecurity of an exiled orphan girl. Praise God that Esther never defined herself that way!

Through the nail-biting tale of Esther, God shows how a woman who defines herself with the right kind of confidence—*inner* confidence in her Lord—relates to others. Instead of listening to what the world said about her, good or bad, Esther derived her confidence from her relationship with God. She had never placed stock in what others felt about her nothingness *or* her queenliness. Esther was confident because she was a *woman of God*. This confidence dramatically affected her relationships with others.

When Mordecai approached Esther to act on behalf of the Jews, she fasted for three days, preparing her heart and her spirit before the Lord. She gathered strength from her relationship with God. And she confidently reported, "I will go to the king, even though it is against the law. And if I perish, I perish" (Esther 4:16).

Esther did not slink into the court after her fast. The Scripture tells us she stood—a mark of confidence—in the king's court (see Esther 5:2). Ultimately, Xerxes not only listened to Esther, but granted her request to protect the Jews.

Because Esther refused to give in to insecurity, she could confidently relate to others—even a powerful king. And because her confidence was the *right* kind—confidence placed in God and not the trappings of beauty, success, or power—she became a fairy-tale heroine for her people.

Esther's confidence defined first her character and then her relationships. Her confidence came from knowing that as a woman of God—a daughter of the King of kings—she was a princess no matter what anyone might say or think.

You may be as beautiful as a queen or as lonely as an orphan. You may enjoy status and prestige, or you may feel as abandoned and worthless as an exile. But none of these things *define* you. When you choose the true confidence that comes with identifying yourself in God, your relationships with others will be marked by success and strength.

Questions for Consideration

1. Up to this point in your life, what things have defined your confidence or lack of confidence?

2. In what ways do you think your self-image influences your relationships with others? Be specific.

3. Read Psalm 71:5. In whom does the psalmist place confidence?

4. Why is God the only place we can find true confidence? (Hint: See Hebrews 13:5-6,8).

5. Read Esther 4:14. Mordecai told Esther that she had "come to royal position for such a time as this." Esther then exhibited the confidence necessary for her to seize the moment. Her relationships with the king and others benefited from the expression of her confidence. If you confidently seized "such a time as this"—the opportunities God has prepared you for—in what ways would your relationships become stronger?

Day 2 (Women): Ruth—Defined by Loyalty

Scriptures: Ruth 1:8-18; 2:11-12; Galatians 5:22-23;
Proverbs 20:6

Thirteen centuries before Christ, things turned sour for the chosen people of God in Judah. The Hebrew nation faced a severe famine, a judgment resulting from their sin and unfaithfulness to the Holy One of Israel.

In these trying times, Jews sought refuge in many places, including distant lands where they thought they could escape God's hand. Elimelech, a man of Bethlehem, took his wife Naomi and two sons, Mahlon and Kilion, to Moab, where he hoped they would fare better than they had in Judah.

Though it was a kingdom full of Baal worshipers, Moab did have fertile ground and ready fields. Moab also provided wives for Elimelech's sons. But these seemingly good things came from a nation tainted by idol worship, from a country with which God had specifically instructed the Israelites not to associate.

Whether or not God judged Elimelech, Mahlon, and Kilion for stepping outside His will, we do not know. But the book of Ruth does record that the three men died within ten years, leaving their mother, Naomi, and their widows, Ruth and Orpah, destitute and abandoned (see Ruth 1:5).

Rather bleak beginnings for a story that turns out to be one of the most refreshing tales of loyalty and love in all written history! In times like ours when human brokenness and the resulting strain commonly choke relationships, the book of Ruth provides a beautiful example of how loyalty—enduring faithfulness and fidelity—redeems not only damaged lives, but broken relationships as well.

We pick up the story after the three widows determined together to return to Naomi's homeland. En route, however, Naomi realized that her daughters-in-law might do no better in Judah than in their own land. She urged them to return to their parents' homes, remarry, and bear children.

Orpah made a dramatic display of love for Naomi—kissing her and weeping—before returning to Moab, to the land of idolatry. But Ruth demonstrated her true loyalty and love not only for her former husband but also for his family and, more important, for the true God. She entreated Naomi, "Don't urge me to leave you or to turn back from you. Where you go I will go, and where you stay I will stay. Your people will be my people and your God my God" (Ruth 1:16).

Ruth had decided to place her faith in Jehovah and would not turn back from Him or the mother-in-law He'd given her. Perhaps Ruth knew what kind of home she would return to in Moab—a family that did not worship Yahweh and that might persecute her for doing so. Because of Ruth's faithfulness to her, Naomi's heart and situation were transformed.

In order to provide for the two women, Ruth gleaned in the fields of her new hometown, working hard in the hot Palestine sun from morning until night. She did so with a glad spirit, anticipating the joy of sharing with her mother-in-law what God provided.

While faithfully serving her mother-in-law, Ruth saw a new strength in her relationship with Naomi. God then presented a great opportunity as a direct result of Ruth's fidelity—the chance to remarry.

Boaz, the wealthy owner of the fields in which Ruth was gleaning, noticed Ruth during her first day on the job. He asked about her (she must have struck his fancy!) and discovered her origins in Moab, her connections to Naomi, and that her diligent labor that day had impressed his workers.

Those field hands must have filled Boaz's ears with praise of Ruth, for he welcomed her to gather in his fields, under his protection, for the duration of the harvest. Boaz offered Ruth this position precisely because he'd heard of her deep loyalty to Naomi and to God. He exclaimed, "May the LORD repay you for what you have done. May you be richly rewarded by the LORD, the God of Israel, under whose wings you have come to take refuge" (Ruth 2:12).

Ruth gleaned in the fields of Boaz for some months and eventually won his heart. Her consistent faithfulness and loyalty impressed Boaz so much that he married her and fathered her first child, a son.

And here's the icing to top it all off: That son, Obed, became King David's grandfather, and none other than Jesus Himself descended from this very line. What amazing blessings resulted from Ruth's decision to remain loyal to her family and to the Lord!

As a woman, you will constantly come to the kinds of crossroads Ruth did. You probably will not have to decide whether to provide for your destitute mother-in-law within the next few years, but you *will* be challenged by circumstances that demand you to choose loyalty or self-service.

Orpah, the other Moabite widow, faded from the pages of Scripture when she chose to place her own needs above faithfulness to others and to God. But Ruth remains immortalized, one of only two women for whom a book of the Bible is named and, more preciously, a great-(times a lot) grandmother of Jesus.

Because of Ruth's loyalty, each of her relationships grew in strength and blessing. God rewarded her faithfulness by providing her with a husband of noble character, a son of distinction, and an intimate love relationship with Naomi.

Our society places little value on loyalty to family, to friends, to God. But as women seeking the Lord, we should make faithfulness a high priority. It is also a fruit of the Holy Spirit dwelling in us. Galatians 5:22-23 reminds us that "love, joy, peace, patience, kindness, goodness, *faithfulness,* gentleness and self-control" (emphasis added) will reveal that we walk in step with the Spirit.

As you choose loyalty, you will see your relationships—with the Lord, with other women, and with men as well—mature and thrive.

Questions for Consideration

1. After reading Ruth's story, define *loyalty*. Look up *loyalty* and *faithfulness* in a dictionary and compare your answers.

2. Proverbs 20:6 tells us, "Many a man proclaims his own loyalty, but who can find a trustworthy man?" (NASB). What lack of loyalty have you seen in the relationships of those around you? in your own relationships?

3. Ruth's name means "friendship." First remaining loyal to her female friendships, Ruth saw her interactions with the opposite sex blessed as well. Do you place high enough value on loyalty to your girlfriends? In other words, do you respect and honor them, or do you often find yourself gossiping, expressing envy, or taking your female relationships for granted when a guy is on your mind? What course of action or attitude adjustments do your answers to these questions suggest?

4. The French playwright Moliere wrote, "Men are alike in their promises. It is only in their deeds that they differ." How true of women as well! We can make all kinds of promises, but unless we follow through with action, ours are empty words. In what ways can you show loyalty through what you *do?* Be specific.

5. In what ways might being loyal to your girlfriends have a positive impact on your ability to maintain healthy relationships with men?

Day 3 (Women): Hannah—Defined by Prayer

Scriptures: I Samuel 1:1–2:11,21; Luke 18:1-8; Psalm 62:8

All too often, we find ourselves praying when the chips are down, when the bottom has dropped out, when there's "nothing more we can do." Yet prayer was never meant to be a last resort. Instead it's to be the first and intermittent stop on every human journey, including the journey of relationships.

John Bunyan, author of *Pilgrim's Progress,* once preached, "You can do more than pray after you have prayed, but you cannot do more than pray until you have prayed." Truly, until we take our needs before God, we can do nothing. We cannot control our circumstances no matter how hard we try.

We cannot overstate the value of defining your character with prayer. In his book *Celebration of Discipline,* Richard Foster wrote,

> Prayer catapults us onto the frontier of the spiritual life. Of all the
> Spiritual Disciplines *prayer is the most central* because it ushers us
> into perpetual communion with the Father.... It is the Discipline
> of prayer that brings us into the deepest and highest work of the
> human spirit. Real prayer is life creating and life changing. [6]

In the book of 1 Samuel, God unveils a shining example of a woman committed to this "perpetual communion with the Father." We see how her faithful intercession created both life and change within her as well as within the people around her.

Hannah stands out as a woman defined by prayer. Married to a polygamous priest in the days when everyone in Israel "did what was right in his own eyes" (Judges 17:6, NASB), Hannah developed a spirit of prayer in an environment that was not conducive to it. The times were against her, and so were her circumstances.

Although her husband was a man committed to worship on one level—Elkanah took his family each year from their home in Ramah to the temple in Shiloh to offer sacrifice and praise—we see no intimate expression of his love relationship with God. Hannah, however, viewed prayer not as a ritual requirement of faith, but as communion with a Person, with the only One who could understand her sorrows and meet her needs.

And Hannah was anguished. Elkanah's other wife, Peninnah, bore him several children, but Hannah's womb remained closed. Not only did she grieve in her own spirit, but she had to endure the ridicules and taunting of the other woman in her home.

Scripture records that during a particularly grueling trip to the temple with the acid-tongued Peninnah, Hannah eventually broke down weeping and refused to eat. But Hannah had learned to take her tears to God. Upon arriving in Shiloh, she immediately retreated to the temple to earnestly pray to the Lord.

It's interesting to contrast Hannah's prayerful response to the trial of childlessness with the reactions of Sarah, Rebekah, and Rachel. Of these four great women of the Bible with initially barren wombs, Hannah alone turned *first* to life-changing prayer. Sarah laughed; Rebekah bore the burden with indolence and coldness; and Rachel became infuriated at waiting so long and cried out: "Give me children, or I'll die!" (Genesis 30:1).

But Hannah prayed. First Samuel 1:15 records that in great sorrow, she poured out her heart to the Lord. After receiving a blessing from Eli the priest, Hannah left the temple with a spirit of peaceful prayer. God had heard. And God answered.

The Lord witnessed Hannah's devotion and opened her womb. She conceived a son and named him Samuel, which means "asked of or heard of the Lord." What an amazing example of how prayer changes not only an attitude, but an entire life.

And Hannah's story did not end there. In fact, we've left out some of the best details! When Samuel came into the world, Hannah composed a prayer of such beauty and sweet communion with her Lord that we see she prayed not only in times of suffering and distress but also in times of thanksgiving and joy.

Prayer also had an impact on Hannah's relationships with others. It must have been no small feat to live with a nasty woman like Peninnah sharing her husband's bed. But a prayerful woman like Hannah is more apt to reflect the heart of God and respond to others in a manner worthy of Him. Never do we witness her retaliating against, or even reacting to, Peninnah. Instead she took her pain to God.

As Hannah prayed through her distress in the temple, Eli mistakenly accused her of drunkenness. When she revealed the truth, this man of God saw the authenticity of her prayerful heart and interceded for her in the name of the Lord. Because prayer had defined Hannah's character, she received this special blessing from the priest.

Finally, her relationships with her family members thrived as a result of her prayerfulness. God filled Hannah's quiver with three more sons and two daughters. And her firstborn, Samuel, served the Lord faithfully all of his days. In fact, he, too, became a person marked and defined by prayer.

Yet we cannot close there. We must share one last piece of Hannah's story: Through prayer, *she* changed. "Prayer is, after all, a very dangerous business. For all the benefits it offers of growing closer to God, it carries with it one great element of risk: the possibility of change. In prayer we open ourselves to the chance that God will do something with us that we have not intended."[7]

The very thing Hannah longed and prayed for most—a son—she surrendered to the Lord. She vowed to God that she would dedicate her son to Him if He would open her womb, and she followed through with her promise. This sacrificial gift of her son makes her prayer of thanksgiving in 1 Samuel that much more poignant and piercing. She praised God for what she would not keep forever. In doing so, she deepened her dependence on God and her love relationship with Him.

Hannah exemplified a spirit defined by prayer. Her story reveals how prayer changes us and creates life in us and those around us. As you seek to develop strong and godly relationships, make sure that prayer—in times of sorrow and in times of joy—marks your character.

Questions for Consideration

1. Hannah and her family had journeyed to Shiloh to worship many times before the events recorded in 1 Samuel took place and God answered her request. This scene was probably not the first time Hannah had prayed for a child. Read the story of the persistent widow in Luke 18:1-8. What do this parable and Hannah's story teach us about bringing our requests before God?

2. In light of Psalm 62:8, why can we confidently pour out our hearts before God and place our trust in Him just as Hannah did?

3. In what ways might a life of continual "poured out" and trusting prayer affect your ability to relate to others? (Think about Hannah's interaction with Peninnah and Eli.)

4. As Richard Foster points out, "To pray is to change. Prayer is the central avenue God uses to transform us. If we are unwilling to change, we will abandon prayer as a noticeable characteristic in our lives."[8] What is your prayer life like? How often do you pray about your relationships? As you begin to pray or as you continue praying about them, listen for what God might want to change in those relationships.

5. Hannah prayed to God and praised Him even when she knew she would hand her son over to lifelong service in the temple. Are you willing to surrender those things or relationships for which you have prayed most fervently? Why or why not?

Day 4 (Women): Mary of Bethany—Defined by Quiet

Scriptures: Luke 10:38-42; 1 Thessalonians 4:11;
1 Peter 3:4; Psalm 46:10

"We live in a noisy, busy world.… We have become a people with an aver-sion to quiet and an uneasiness with being alone."[9] Our schedules reflect a frenetic, frantic pace that is anything but quiet and contemplative. We fill our life with noise from every angle—loud music and flashing images, even the deafening chaos of perpetual interaction with others. Our society avoids silence and generally perceives being alone as repugnant.

Yet busyness and noise decimate relationships. They cause us to sub-stitute shallow activity for deep unity. Christ calls us away from the frenzy so that we might commune with Him and authentically love and relate to others.

In Luke 10, the Lord gives us a brief glimpse into the life of a woman who knew the value of quiet. In fact, Mary of Bethany defined her char-acter by calmly abiding in her Lord's presence. And she did so amidst the temptation to rush to accomplish.

The short account of Jesus' visit to Bethany records that Mary and her sister Martha welcomed the Lord into their home. Scripture reveals very little about the time they spent together. We do know for certain, how-ever, that Martha bustled around while Mary sat quietly at the Lord's feet, hanging on His every word.

And we further discover that Martha became agitated by Mary's calm contemplation. Martha approached Jesus and casually mentioned (we're being nice here!) that it didn't seem fair that she should do all the work while Mary sat in what she saw as quiet carelessness.

But Jesus responded with basically these words, "Martha, dear Martha, you're fussing far too much and getting yourself worked up over nothing.

One thing only is essential, and Mary has chosen it—it's the main course, and won't be taken from her" (Luke 10:41-42, MSG). Jesus spoke with neither vindictiveness nor judgment. He loved Martha. He knew that she loved Him (see John 11). But she'd allowed the busyness and noise of her activities—done to facilitate fellowship with the Lord!—to crowd out what was really important. She placed a higher emphasis on accomplishing the task at hand than she did on communing with Christ.

Now a dinner of some kind did have to be prepared. And the house most likely needed to be made ready to accommodate Jesus, possibly overnight. But Martha allowed these details to consume not only her time but her energy and her spirit as well. Mary quietly chose to sit at Jesus' feet, and Christ called this "what is better" (Luke 10:42).

As a woman today, you constantly face the pressures of noise and busyness. Some of the things crowding your schedule you *have* to do. Yet there are other things you choose. In making your choices, are you pursuing a life that includes time for quietly sitting at Jesus' feet?

In this instance, Martha defined her character with accomplishment, with busyness. As a result, she became frustrated in her relationships with others—especially her calm sister. Mary, on the other hand, chose to define her character with quiet, and she could love the Lord and others with sensitivity and compassion. We see this elsewhere in Scripture, as when Mary interacts with Jesus and with her brother and sister. (For further reading, see John 12:1-3 and notice how Mary helps her sister care for and celebrate her brother, as well as how she lavishes love on Jesus.)

The apostle Paul exhorted all Christians to "make it your ambition to lead a quiet life" (1 Thessalonians 4:11). Sometimes developing a quiet life means saying no to frantic scheduling; sometimes it involves choosing to be alone when you could be with others. You could easily fill your schedule not merely with activity, but with opportunities for fellowship.

But a bow that's constantly bent *will* break, as the ancient Greek saying goes. And a woman who's constantly busy and continually with others *will* see her relationships suffer.

The fruit of solitude is increased sensitivity and compassion for others. There comes a new freedom to be with people. There is a new attentiveness to their needs, a new responsiveness to their hurts. Thomas Merton observes, "It is in deep solitude that I find the gentleness with which I can truly love my brothers."[10]

As you define your character, choose—as Mary did—"what is better": "the unfading beauty of a gentle and *quiet* spirit, which is of great worth in God's sight" (1 Peter 3:4, emphasis added). Take time for quiet and solitude, and you will see your relationships flourish in beautiful ways. In a noisy, busy world, this invitation is a fantastic challenge but one that offers great reward.

Questions for Consideration

1. According to Jesus, Mary chose "what is better." Why is a quiet character better than a busy, noisy one?

2. Take a moment to evaluate your schedule and lifestyle. In what ways can you "make it your ambition to lead a quiet[er] life" (1 Thessalonians 4:11)?

3. How comfortable are you with silence? How do you feel about being alone?

4. Reflect on Psalm 46:10. Why does being still help define a person's relationship with God? Why will a more clearly defined relationship with God, in turn, help you define your relationships with others?

5. Dietrich Bonhoeffer wrote, "Let him [or her] who cannot be
    alone beware of community.... One who wants fellowship
    without solitude plunges into the world of words and feel-
    ings."[11] Why would plunging "into the world of words and
    feelings" hinder your ability to clearly define your relation-
    ships with the opposite sex? Specifically, in what ways might
    it affect your ability to guard your heart?

DAY 5 (WOMEN): SARAH—DEFINED BY MEEKNESS

*Scriptures: Genesis 11:31–12:5; 16:1-4; 17:15-17; 18:1-15;
and 21:1-7; 1 Peter 3:4,6; Matthew 5:5*

We'll bet a lot of people out there don't know what to make of the word
meekness. Some people might immediately be turned off, assuming that it
means "weak."

Yet the Bible describes Jesus Himself as "meek in spirit" (see 2 Corinthians 10:1), and we know that He had divine strength and power. The
Lord promises that the *meek* "will inherit the earth" (Matthew 5:5). And
1 Peter 3:4 exhorts all women to develop a "meek and quiet spirit" (KJV).
We'd better figure out what this word really means since God clearly wants
meekness to mark our character.

The basic idea behind meekness is great strength under control. The
visual image associated with meekness is a powerful animal taught, tamed,
and controlled by a wise and caring master. Meekness implies a willing
submission to someone in order to learn and to obey.

First Peter 3 names one woman who exemplified meekness. A woman
of "meek and quiet spirit," Sarah ultimately submitted to her God and to
her husband. Peter records that "you are her daughters if you do what is
right and do not give way to fear" (1 Peter 3:6). Jill Briscoe asks, "So what

does the Bible mean when it call us to be daughters of Sarah?… It calls us to emulate her basic attitude of cooperation with God, allowing Him a chance to change us."[12]

Sarah's life started as no ideal illustration of willing submission. A feisty woman of definite ideas and proven competence, the young Sarah knew how to get things done. Thinking her strength could carry her, she ran ahead of the Lord and her husband. Sarah had to *learn* and *choose* meekness.

As women of the twenty-first century, groomed to define ourselves by our power and strength, we, too, must become skilled at submission and make the choice to be meek.

Two instances from Sarah's life highlight how she chose and learned meekness. The first occurs in Genesis 11 and 12, where we witness God calling Sarah's husband, Abram, to leave his home and "go to the land I will show you" (Genesis 12:1).

At this time Sarah was a different person than the meek and quiet spirit Peter later described. In fact, her name was Sarai, derived from the same Hebrew root as "striving or contentious."

We can imagine that hearing she would leave country, family, and comforts in order to live nomadically in an unknown land did *not* please the fiery Sarai. But she chose to follow, to submit to the Lord and the husband He had placed in her life.

For this, God rewarded her with a new name, Sarah, which means "princess." Because she chose to believe God and follow His lead through Abram, Sarah received not only an exalted title, but also the promise that God would make her the mother of many nations.

Exactly how did Sarah learn meekness? Through that promise itself. In Genesis 16 Sarah took matters into her own hands and tried to hasten God's promise by encouraging her husband to father a child with her maid. Sarah's attempt to manipulate God went sour.

But God again granted Sarah the chance to learn submission and to allow Him to harness her strength under His control. In chapters 18 and 21 we see Sarah change from a woman who laughed at God's promise to a woman who has learned to trust in His faithfulness. God not only blessed an aged (and we're talking over *ninety years old!*) Sarah with a son but with joy in her circumstances. As she learned to yield to the Lord, she reveled in the benefits of submitting her strength to Him.

As you can see, a meek spirit equals a submissive spirit. You may have heard teaching on submission and been confused by the whole thing. We pray that looking at how Sarah defined her character with meekness— strength under control and willing obedience—will help give you a better picture of what submission looks like.

At one time, I (Jerusha) wrongly supposed that submission and leadership were opposites. Learning what meekness meant and how Sarah exemplified it, I discovered that submission and manipulation are the true opposites. The choice is not between leading and submitting but between submitting or maneuvering for your own way.

Sarah learned that manipulation not only could not get her what she wanted but kept her from real relationship with the Lord and others. In Genesis 16, we read how her unsubmissive act of giving Hagar to sleep with Abraham led to dissension in her home, in her marriage, and in her walk with God. Only in meekness was Sarah released to truly love others.

Richard Foster wrote,

> The freedom submission brings is the ability to lay down the terrible burden of always needing to get our own way.... In submission we are free at last to value other people. Their dreams and plans become important to us. We have entered into a new, wonderful, glorious freedom—the freedom to give up our own rights for the good of others.[13]

A meek spirit yields to God first and then to the people he has placed in our lives. A submissive heart does not seek its own way, but willingly surrenders power and control. If you develop a character of meekness during the years you date, your relationships—with God and with others—will thrive both now and later. (If you are interested in more information on submission—particularly between men and women—we recommend you look at P. B. Wilson's book *Liberated Through Submission,* published by Harvest House.)

Questions for Consideration

1. After reading about Sarah, describe meekness and submission.

2. Why do you think these two concepts are given a bad rap in our society?

3. Why do you think God might be calling you to learn and to choose meekness in your life right now?

4. As you become skilled at yielding to God and others—as you stop demanding your own way—in what ways might your relationships with men mature and change?

5. What have you heard about submission in marriage? In what ways do the truths you learned from Sarah's life confirm or change what you thought?

Notes

Introduction

1. Ed Wheat, *Love Life for Every Married Couple,* quoted in Nick Harrison, *Promises to Keep* (New York: HarperSanFrancisco, 1996), 54.
2. Gary Chapman, *The Five Love Languages* (Chicago: Northfield, 1995), 35, emphasis added.
3. Chapman, *Love Languages,* 131, emphasis added.

Chapter One

1. Len Woods, *The Unofficial Guide to Life After High School* (Grand Rapids, Mich.: Baker, 1998), 74.
2. Dwight Edwards, *Revolution Within* (Colorado Springs: Water-Brook, 2000), 44.
3. C. S. Lewis, *Mere Christianity* (New York: Macmillan, 1952), 120.
4. Augustine once wrote, "There is a God-shaped hole in the human spirit…a vacuum that must be filled." And Blaise Pascal wrote, "There is a God-shaped vacuum in the heart of every man which cannot be filled by any created thing, but only by God the Creator, made known through Jesus Christ."
5. Henry Blackaby and Claude V. King, *Experiencing God* (Nashville: Broadman & Holman, 1994), 11-2.
6. Ruth Myers, *The Satisfied Heart* (Colorado Springs: WaterBrook, 1999), 180.
7. Woods, *Unofficial Guide,* 68.
8. Stephen Arterburn and Jack Felton, *Toxic Faith* (Nashville: Oliver-Nelson, 1991), 31.
9. Oswald Chambers, *My Utmost for His Highest* (Grand Rapids, Mich.: Discovery House, 1992), May 12 entry.

Chapter Two

1. Wes Roberts and H. Norman Wright, *Before You Say, "I Do"* (Eugene, Oreg.: Harvest House, 1978), 52.
2. Roberts and Wright, *"I Do,"* 53-4.
3. Wayne A. Mack, *Preparing for Marriage God's Way* (Tulsa, Okla.: Hensley, 1994), 65.
4. H. Dale Burke, *Different by Design* (Chicago: Moody, 2000), 157.
5. Chapman, *Love Languages,* 61.
6. P. B. Wilson, *Knight in Shining Armor* (Eugene, Oreg.: Harvest House, 1995), 155.
7. Gary Rosberg, *Do-It-Yourself* (Colorado Springs: Focus on the Family, 1999), 182.
8. Chapman, *Love Languages,* 97.
9. Chapman, *Love Languages,* 92.
10. For some of the ideas in this section, we are indebted to Laurie Polich, of Youth Specialties, whose talk on love at Winterfest 2002 inspired us to include examples of each of the ways "love" is described.

Chapter Three

1. Rosberg, *Do-It-Yourself,* 205.

Chapter Four

1. In our book, *He's HOT, She's HOT* (WaterBrook), we spend a good deal of time developing how you become such a person of character, a person worth being desired and pursued. If this idea is new to you, we suggest that you check out the chapter "Becoming What You Want."
2. If you're unclear what a boundary is or what healthy physical and emotional boundaries look like, we'd like to refer you to another book we wrote, *I Gave Dating a Chance* (WaterBrook). In chapters 9 and 10 we deal specifically with physical and emotional limits.

Chapter Five

1. Anne Morrow Lindbergh, quoted in Charles Swindoll, *Tale of the Tardy Oxcart* (Dallas: Word, 1998), 478.

2. Charles Swindoll, *Growing Strong in the Seasons of Life* (Grand Rapids, Mich.: Multnomah, 1983), 138.
3. Burke, *Design,* 152.
4. Rosberg, *Do-it-Yourself,* 5-6.
5. Wilson, *Knight,* 93.
6. Josh McDowell, *The Teenage Q&A* (Dallas: Word, 1990), 162.

Chapter Six
1. Antoine de Saint-Exupéry, quoted in Art Hunt, *Praying with the One You Love* (Sisters, Oreg.: Multnomah, 1996), 12.
2. Adapted from David and Heather Kopp, *Praying the Bible for Your Marriage* (Colorado Springs: WaterBrook, 1997), 83.
3. Samuel Dickey Gordon, quoted in L. B. Cowman, *Streams in the Desert* (Grand Rapids, Mich.: Zondervan, 1999), 314.
4. Cowman, *Streams,* 194.
5. Cowman, *Streams,* 472.

Chapter Seven
1. Swindoll, *Growing Strong,* 163.
2. Aleksandr Solzhenitsyn, quoted in *God's Little Instruction Book for Graduates* (Colorado Springs: Honor, 1994), 229.
3. Cowman, *Streams,* 109.
4. Swindoll, *Growing Strong,* 315.
5. Richard Foster, *Celebration of Discipline* (San Francisco: HarperCollins, 1988), 198.
6. Adolph Coors, quoted in Harrison, *Promises,* 49.
7. Dwight Carlson, *Overcoming Hurts and Anger* (Eugene, Oreg.: Harvest House, 1981), 126.
8. Lewis Smedes, *Forgive and Forget* (New York: Simon and Schuster, 1984), 45.
9. Swindoll, *Growing Strong,* 232-3.
10. Jerry Bridges, *On Trusting God* (Colorado Springs: NavPress, 1988), 177.
11. Chambers, *My Utmost,* January 13 entry, emphasis added.
12. Cowman, *Streams,* 409.

CHAPTER EIGHT

1. Jeramy Clark, *I Gave Dating a Chance* (Colorado Springs: WaterBrook, 2000), 101.
2. Foster, *Celebration*, 101.
3. P. D. James, *Death in Holy Orders* (New York: Knopf, 2001), 237-8.
4. Some great Christian resources are available if you suspect that gender differences may be hindering your relationships. Look for the books and tapes of Dr. Gary Smalley at your local Christian bookstore. His material can give you a good start in taking into account the differences between men and women.
5. Gregg Jantz, *Too Close to the Flame* (West Monroe, La.: Howard, 1999), 142.

CHAPTER NINE

1. Stephen Arterburn and Fred Stoeker, *Every Young Man's Battle* (Colorado Springs: WaterBrook, 2002), 2.
2. Stephen Klotz, "Sex in the Cafeteria," *Group*, Jan/Feb 2002, 37.
3. Jantz, *Flame*, 8.
4. Lorraine Ali and Julie Scelfo, "Choosing Virginity," 62, and Debra Rosenberg, "The Battle Over Abstinence," 68, *Newsweek*, 9 December 2002.
5. Dennie Hughes, "The Sex Lives of Kids," *USA Weekend: The Denver Post and Rocky Mountain News Edition*, 23-25 August 2002, 7.
6. Jantz, *Flame*, 3.
7. Centers for Disease Control and Prevention. See www.cdc.gov for comprehensive listings.
8. Focus on the Family, *No Apologies: The Truth About Life, Love, and Sex* (Wheaton, Ill.: Tyndale, 1999), 104.
9. *Time*, 6 August 2001, quoted in *Youthworker*.
10. *lovematters.com* magazine, supplement, vol. 2 (Redondo Beach, Calif.: LoveMatters.com, 2001), 2.
11. Focus on the Family, *No Apologies*, 90.
12. Elton Trueblood, quoted in Focus on the Family, *No Apologies*, 166-7.
13. Some resources you can investigate are *Gift-Wrapped by God* (Linda Dillow and Lorraine Pintus, WaterBrook), which will be particu-

larly helpful to the women out there, and Josh Harris's book *Not Even a Hint* (Multnomah). Also extraordinarily helpful is *Every Young Man's Battle* (Stephen Arterburn and Fred Stoeker, WaterBrook).

14. These ideas are adapted from those found in *No Apologies.*
15. Bruce Larson, *There's a Lot More to Health Than Not Being Sick* (Dallas: Word, 1981), quoted in Swindoll, *Tale of the Tardy Oxcart,* 10, emphasis added.

CHAPTER TEN

1. Lewis, *Mere Christianity,* 64.
2. Eugene Peterson, *Leap over a Wall* (New York: HarperSanFrancisco, 1997), 53-5.
3. Jack Hayford, quoted in Harrison, *Promises,* 34-5.
4. Chambers, *My Utmost,* March 19 entry.
5. Jerry Bridges, *The Practice of Godliness* (Colorado Springs: NavPress, 1994), 92.
6. Foster, *Celebration,* 33, emphasis added.
7. Emilie Griffin, quoted in David and Heather Kopp, *Praying the Bible,* 57.
8. Foster, *Celebration,* 33.
9. Jean Fleming, *Finding Focus in a Whirlwind World* (Fort Collins, Colo.: Through the Bible, 1991), 73.
10. Foster, *Celebration,* 108.
11. Dietrich Bonhoeffer, *Life Together* (New York: Harper and Row, 1952), 77-8.
12. Jill Briscoe, *Women Who Changed Their World* (Colorado Springs: ChariotVictor, 1991), 24.
13. Foster, *Celebration,* 111-2.

About the Authors

Jeramy and Jerusha Clark first served together in youth ministry at the First Evangelical Free Church of Fullerton, California. Prior to that, Jeramy worked in student ministries at the Church at Rocky Peak and Valley Bible Church, both in California. He earned his bachelor's degree from The Master's College and a master's of divinity degree from Talbot Seminary. Jerusha is a graduate of Rice University.

After meeting in Fullerton, Jeramy and Jerusha dated and eventually married. They ministered at Tri-Lakes Chapel in Monument, Colorado, for over four years. Their best-selling book, *I Gave Dating a Chance,* offers a biblical perspective to balance the extremes of dating and courtship, while their second book, *He's HOT, She's HOT,* focuses on one of the most crucial aspects of healthy dating and marriage: choosing a godly companion.

Jeramy and Jerusha live with their two daughters in Escondido, California, where Jeramy pastors five hundred high-school students at Emmanuel Faith Community Church.

**Ken thinks he and Becky are just having fun together.
Becky is already picking out bridesmaid dresses.**

**Melissa has decided to break up with Tony.
Tony thinks Melissa is "the one."**

*Are miscommunications like this unavoidable?
What's the best way to end a relationship—or to take it to a more serious level?*

Chances are, you've heard of "The Talk." Every romantic relationship comes to the point where things need to be defined or redefined: Do we become romantically exclusive? Is our relationship ready (or not ready) to move to the next level? What are our boundaries and expectations? Is it possible to "just be friends"?

Getting all the cards on the table. Communicating openly and honestly. It sounds like a great idea, right? The tough question is, how do you communicate in a way that significantly benefits you both—and doesn't leave you dreading those important conversations in the future?

In *Define the Relationship,* you'll find everything you need to know about positively defining and redefining your current or future dating relationships. Written in light of the complexities of dating today, this long-needed resource will help you avoid painful and confusing dating dilemmas and experience instead the freedom of well-defined, spiritually grounded, and truly rewarding relationships.

"Define the Relationship takes a refreshing approach to dating by shining light on the subtle pitfalls couples face today.… Jeramy and Jerusha Clark fill a huge vacuum in Christian resources on dating by writing this book."
—DR. LORI SALIERNO, speaker, author, and founder of Celebrate Life International

---

Jeramy and Jerusha Clark are the authors of the best-selling *I Gave Dating a Chance* and *He's H.O.T., She's H.O.T.* They live with their two daughters in Escondido, California, where Jeramy pastors high school students at Emmanuel Faith Community Church.

COVER DESIGN: JOHN HAMILTON
COVER PHOTOGRAPHY: STONE/PHILIP LEE HARVEY

DATING / CHRISTIAN LIVING

US $12.99 / $19.99 CAN
ISBN 1-57856-592-8

51299

9 781578 565924

958785
ARK
DEFINETHER
CLSL   1204

$12.99
FAMILY
CHRISTIAN STORES

WATERBROOK PRESS

Visit our Web site at www.w